VISTAS CULTURALES

Video Guide

PEARSON
Prentice
Hall

woRLd
Languages

Upper Saddle River, New Jersey 07458

Senior Media Editor: Samantha Alducin
Supplements Editor: Meriel Martinez Moctezuma
Project Manager: Jill Traut
Production Editor: Manuel Echevarria
Asst. Director of Production: Mary Rottino
Prepress and Manufacturing Buyer: Christina Amato
Prepress and Manufacturing Asst. Manager: Mary Ann Gloriande
Cover Art Director: Jayne Conte
Cover Design: Bruce Kenselaar
Publisher: Phil Miller

This book was set in 10/12 Palatino by the Interactive Composition Corporation and was printed and bound by RRD-Harrisonburg. The cover was printed by RRD-Harrisonburg.

Copyright © 2007 by Pearson Education, Inc.
Upper Saddle River, NJ 07458

Printed in the United States of America
10 9 8 7 6 5 4 3 2 1

ISBN 0-13-158917-2

Pearson Education LTD., *London*
Pearson Education Australia PTY, Limited, *Sydney*
Pearson Education Singapore, Pte. Ltd
Pearson Education North Asia Ltd., *Hong Kong*
Pearson Education Canada, Ltd., *Toronto*
Pearson Educación de México, S.A. de C.V.
Pearson Education–Japan, *Tokyo*
Pearson Education Malaysia, Pte. Ltd
Pearson Education, *Upper Saddle River*, New Jersey

Contents

El mundo hispano

INTRODUCTION

The video segment you are about to watch is an introduction to the **Mundo hispano** and the **Vistas culturales** series, a video tour of Spain and Latin America. Although all of these videos are narrated in Spanish, this introductory segment is in English. As you watch this introduction, we hope you will gain a preliminary understanding of the richness and diversity of the cultures of Spanish-speaking countries, and that you will share our enthusiasm about the virtual journey ahead.

I. Before Viewing

1-1. Where is Spanish spoken? Working with a partner, and without consulting any map or textbook, make a list of all of the countries you can think of where Spanish is spoken as a primary language. To make this task a little easier, categorize these by region: Europe, the Caribbean, North America, Central America, South America.

1-2. Other languages of the Americas. Contrary to what some people believe, Spanish is not the official language of the Caribbean, Central American, and South American countries listed below. Indicate which language from the list to the right is spoken in each of these countries.

1. _____ Jamaica   **a.** French
2. _____ Haiti   **b.** English
3. _____ The Bahamas   **c.** Dutch
4. _____ Curaçao   **d.** Portuguese
5. _____ Belize
6. _____ Guyana
7. _____ Suriname
8. _____ French Guyana
9. _____ Brazil

2-1. Comprehension. The following sentences contain information mentioned in the video segment you are about to watch. They are organized chronologically. Read through the sentences so that you know what to listen for and then, as you are watching the video, complete the sentences.

1. The reason the United States is included in this video series is that

   _________________________.

2. The famous Running of the Bulls is also called the _____________________ and it takes place in _____________________.

3. Appetizers served in little portions in bars all over Spain are called

   _________________.

4. What we know as "Spanish" is called _________________ in Spain.

5. The native people of the Caribbean were the _____________________.

6. In the country of _________________, indigenous people are in the majority, but in _________________, _________________, _________________, _________________, _________________ and _________________ they are large minorities.

7. If you don't understand something that the narrator says in Spanish in one of the segments, you should _____________________________________

   _____________________________________.

8. Two things you can say in Spanish when someone is about to go somewhere are _____________________________________

   _____________________________________.

III. After Viewing

3-1. Comparisons. One section of the video focuses on the presence of indigenous people and culture in Latin America, despite their conquest 500 years ago. With a partner, discuss the similarities and differences between the Spanish conquest of Latin America and the colonial period of your own country or region. Then you will be asked to share your insights with the rest of the class. Use the following questions as a guide:

- Who lived there before European colonizers arrived?
- When did the Europeans arrive?
- What happened during the conquest?
- What happened to the conquered people?
- What influence does the culture(s) of the conquered people have on the majority culture today?
- What cultural site(s) do you know of that were built by the indigenous people who lived in this place before the Europeans arrived?

3-2. Traveling to *El mundo hispano*. Imagine that you have been promised a scholarship to travel to the Spanish-speaking country of your choice and to spend one month there studying Spanish and learning about the country's culture. From what you learned during this brief segment, and any additional information you may have gathered firsthand or from your studies, choose the country you would travel to and write a paragraph about what you would like to do there and why that country interests you.

Argentina

INTRODUCTION

This video presents basic information about Argentina, a very large country in South America with many interesting places to visit. Get ready to enjoy the trip!

USEFUL VOCABULARY

cataratas	*waterfalls*	estilo	*style*
paisaje	*landscape*	barrio	*neighborhood*
feria	*fair*	cascada	*waterfall*
cosmopolita	*cosmopolitan*	bosque	*forest*
edificio	*building*	desierto	*desert*

I. Before Viewing

1-1. Datos sobre Argentina. Indicate below what you already know about Argentina by answering the following questions in Spanish.

1. ¿Dónde está situado Argentina?

2. ¿Cómo es este país?

3. ¿Cuáles son algunas comidas típicas?

4. ¿Cuál es una actividad preferida de los argentinos?

1-2. Consulta en internet. Consult the Internet to find out the significance of the following words. Each is related somehow to Argentina.

1. el tango
2. las Pampas
3. el gaucho
4. Buenos Aires
5. el río de la Plata

II. While Viewing

2-1. Cierto o falso. As you watch the video, read the sentences and decide if they are true **(Cierto)** or false **(Falso)**.

	Cierto	Falso
1. Argentina está ubicada en América del Sur.	☐	☐
2. Purmamarca es un pueblito de la provincia de Misiones.	☐	☐
3. Las Ruinas de San Ignacio Miní fueron construidas por los jesuitas.	☐	☐
4. Buenos Aires es la ciudad capital de Argentina.	☐	☐
5. Los inmigrantes alemanes vivieron en La Boca.	☐	☐
6. El Glaciar Perito Moreno está en el sur de Argentina.	☐	☐
7. Toman mate en el desayuno y la merienda.	☐	☐
8. Los argentinos comen pastas frescas.	☐	☐

2-2. **Amigos viajeros.** Read the conversations between friends to see if you can guess to which places in Argentina they are referring.

Conversación 1

CARLA: Esta ciudad es muy grande. Hay mucha gente y es ruidosa.
EUGENIA: Pero es muy bonita. Tiene edificios modernos y antiguos.
CARLA: Prefiero una ciudad más tranquila.
EUGENIA: A mí me gusta esta ciudad.

LUGAR: ____

Conversación 2

AGUSTINA: ¡Qué frío! Debí traer más ropa abrigada para el frío.
MATÍAS: Sí, trajiste poca ropa abrigada. Yo traje guantes, gorro, bufanda y
           medias bien calientitas.
AGUSTINA: Sí, hice mal, ahora no puedo disfrutar de este lugar tan bonito y con
           tanto hielo.

LUGAR: ____

2-3. **¿Qué palabras se usan?** Watch the video again. Complete the paragraph with the following words.

tradicional	mate	agua caliente
yerba	bombilla	

El mate es una bebida _________________ (1) en Argentina. Se usa un _________________ (2) en donde se pone la _________________ (3) y se usa la _________________ (4) para tomarlo. Se llena el mate con _________________ (5).

III. After Viewing

3-1. **Me gusta Argentina.** Answer the following questions about Argentina in Spanish.

1. ¿Cómo son Argentina y su gente?

2. ¿Qué lugar de Argentina te interesó más? ¿Por qué?

3. ¿Conoces algún lugar en los Estados Unidos que se parezca a alguno de los lugares que viste? ¿Cuál es ese lugar?

3-2. Las comidas de Argentina. Answer the following questions.

1. De la comida argentina, ¿qué plato parece el más delicioso?

2. ¿Qué comida no quieres probar?

3. ¿Qué plato te gustaría preparar?

3-3. La vida nocturna. Write three sentences in Spanish to compare nightlife in your country with nightlife in Argentina.

Vida nocturna en Argentina	Vida nocturna en: _____

3-4. Carta a un amigo. Write a letter in Spanish to a friend inviting him or her to visit Argentina with you. In your letter tell your friend about things to do and places to see. You may start your letter with *Querido/a* . . . (Dear . . .) and close it with *Un abrazo de* . . . (With a hug from . . .), or any other appropriate salutation and closing.

IV. Class Activities

4-1. Crucigrama en grupos. In the video you learned about some Argentinean foods. Use the information from the video, as well as research from the Internet, to complete the puzzle.

Horizontales (*Across*)

2. Se compra en la carnicería.
3. Bebida muy famosa en Argentina.
4. Lo que se pone adentro del mate.
7. Rellenas (*filled*) con carne o con queso y jamón o con cebollas. Se comen con la mano.
9. Ejemplo de la influencia de inmigrantes italianos.
10. Lo que se usa para tomar el mate.

Verticales (*Down*)

  1. Panes dulces que se comen con el desayuno o la merienda.

  5. Galletas rellenas de dulce de leche y cubiertas de chocolate.

  6. Se compran en la verdulería.

  8. Carne a la parrilla.

4-2. **Vamos de paseo a...** Consult the Internet to find more information about other places in Argentina. Choose a place that interests you and prepare a brief report in Spanish for the class that includes information about that place's geography and activities.

Bolivia y Paraguay

INTRODUCTION

You are going to view a video with information about two South American countries: Bolivia, a country of many unique contrasts, and Paraguay, a bilingual country where Spanish is spoken along with **Guaraní**, the language of its original inhabitants. You will learn about the history, landscape, and environment, as well as the economy, music, food, and celebrations of these two countries.

To complete some of the exercises below you will need to view the video as directed: all at once, individually, and/or without the volume.

USEFUL VOCABULARY

BOLIVIA

Geografía

Lago Titicaca	*Lake Titicaca*
sudeste	*southeast*
suroeste	*southwest*
sobre el nivel del mar	*above sea level*
Misiones Jesuíticas	*Jesuit Missions*

Productos, música y comidas

gas natural	*natural gas*
cañas de bambú	*bamboo canes*
concha de caracol	*snail shell*

PARAGUAY

Geografía e historia

sin costas	*landlocked*
río	*river*
selva	*jungle*
bosque	*forest*
mestizo	*of Spanish and indigenous origin*
guaraní	*original inhabitants, the language they spoke*
Misiones Jesuíticas	*Jesuit missions*
guerra	*war*
stronato	*Stroessner's dictatorship in Paraguay*
caída	*fall*
oriental	*eastern*
occidental	*western*
llanuras	*plains*
salto de agua	*waterfall*

Productos y comidas

yerba mate	*mate, a Paraguayan herbal tea*
riqueza	*wealth*
recursos minerales	*mineral resources*
hidrografía	*hydrography*
mandioca	*yucca root*
maíz	*corn*
soyo	*soup made of ground meat*
mbeju	*tortilla made of yucca flour and cheese*
tereré	*cold yerba mate drink*
hierbas	*herbs*

Palabras relacionadas con el bilingüismo

jopará	*mixed language (Guaraní and Spanish)*
che ra'a	*my friend (literally, my image)*
piko	*interrogative particle borrowed from Guaraní*
so'o	*meat*
avati	*corn*
ka'a	*yerba mate*

Música y artesanías

guarania	*a type of melodic and nostalgic music*
danza de la botella	*dance of the bottle*
chopo	*a Paraguayan dance*
ñandutí	*handmade lace patterned like a spider web*
aho po'i	*hand-embroidered textiles*

I. Before Viewing

1-1. Basic facts about Bolivia. Consult the Internet and/or an encyclopedia to help you answer the following questions about Bolivia.

    1. Where is Bolivia located? Name four countries that share a border with Bolivia.

    2. Who was the hero of Bolivia's independence from Spain?

    3. What do Bolivia and Paraguay have in common because of their location?

    4. Name the highest navigable lake in the world, shared by Bolivia and Peru.

    5. For whom was Bolivia named?

1-2. What do you know about Paraguay? List five topics related to Paraguay that are of interest to you or about which you are curious. Then, watch the video segment on Paraguay with the volume turned off.

II. While Viewing

2-1. De todo un poco sobre Bolivia. Watch the introductory segment of the video on Bolivia and indicate if the sentences below are true (**Cierto**) or false (**Falso**) based on what you see and hear and have learned from the video. Correct any false statements.

    1. Bolivia tiene dos capitales, La Paz y Sucre.

       ❏ **Cierto**   ❏ **Falso**

    ____

    2. El gas natural es uno de los recursos naturales de Bolivia.

       ❏ **Cierto**   ❏ **Falso**

    ____

3. Simón Bolívar es también conocido como El Libertador.

☐ **Cierto**   ☐ **Falso**

____

4. Bolivia tiene cuatro idiomas oficiales, incluyendo el inglés.

☐ **Cierto**   ☐ **Falso**

____

5. El actual presidente de Bolivia es mestizo.

☐ **Cierto**   ☐ **Falso**

____

6. Bolivia tiene puertos marítimos.

☐ **Cierto**   ☐ **Falso**

____

7. La Paz es la capital más alta del mundo.

☐ **Cierto**   ☐ **Falso**

____

8. La música boliviana es conocida en el mundo como música andina.

☐ **Cierto**   ☐ **Falso**

____

2-2. **Patrimonio histórico boliviano.** Select the correct expression on the right to complete the ideas expressed on the left side of the chart.

1	La historia de Bolivia está marcada por numerosas . . .		. . . es un indio aymara.
2	Simón Bolívar . . .		. . . el presidente Morales.
3	Está actualmente luchando por más autonomía sobre los recursos naturales . . .		. . . el petróleo y el gas natural.
4	El presidente Evo Morales . . .		. . . fue el héroe de la independencia de Bolivia.
5	Unos recursos naturales en Bolivia son . . .		. . . dictaduras militares.

2-3. **De todo un poco sobre Paraguay.** Watch the introductory segment of the video on Paraguay and indicate if the sentences below are true (**Cierto**) or false (**Falso**) based on what you see and hear and have learned from the video. Correct any false statements.

    1. El Paraguay es un país marítimo porque limita con Bolivia, Argentina y Brasil.

    ❐ **Cierto**   ❐ **Falso**

    ____

    2. La mayor parte de la población es una mezcla de españoles y guaraníes.

    ❐ **Cierto**   ❐ **Falso**

    ____

    3. Los mestizos del Paraguay no hablan guaraní.

    ❐ **Cierto**   ❐ **Falso**

    ____

    4. El idioma guaraní sobrevivió porque los españoles fueron muy buenos con los indígenas.

    ❐ **Cierto**   ❐ **Falso**

    ____

    5. El mate y la lengua guaraní son elementos únicos de la cultura paraguaya.

    ❐ **Cierto**   ❐ **Falso**

    ____

2-4. **Paisajes, clima y arterias paraguayos.**
Paso 1. Watch the video segment about climate and landscape and complete the following sentences according to the information you see and hear. You may view the video more than once if necessary.

    1. El Paraguay se llama así por _________________________________.

    2. La vegetación del Gran Chaco es _________________________________.

    3. El río Paraná se encuentra en _________________________________.

    4. Las selvas están en la Región _________________________________.

Paso 2. Watch the video segment about the Paraguayan landscape again. Then, imagine you are visiting Paraguay and write a postcard to a family member or friend describing the river you have just seen in the video.

2-4. La comida. Watch the video segment on **La comida** and then, with a classmate, list five Paraguayan foods or beverages that are mentioned. Then, indicate which of these food items are similar or different from American foods and indicate the reasons for the similarities and differences. You may consult the Internet or encyclopedias to find more information on this topic.

2-5. Artesanías, música y atracciones turísticas. Watch the video segment on handicrafts. Now explain what **ñandutí** is to someone who has never seen this craft before.

<h2 style="background:black;color:white;padding:4px 10px;display:inline-block">III. After Viewing</h2>

3-1. El Presidente Morales. The day before President Evo Morales, an Aymara native, was sworn into office he was declared **Apu Mallku** (Supreme Leader) by the Aymara people. President Morales is the country's first indigenous head of state since the Spanish Conquest over 450 years ago. More than 60% of Bolivia's population is indigenous, although not all Aymara. (Consult the Internet or an encyclopedia to complete the activity below.)

1. In what South American countries is the Aymara population present?
2. What percentage of Bolivia's population is Aymara? Where are they located?
3. What would be the equivalent of *Apu Mallku* in one of America's native cultures?

3-2. El guaraní en el Paraguay y el mundo. One of the distinguishing aspects of Paraguayan culture is its extended bilingualism. How is this different or similar to the linguistic situation in the United States?

Paso 1. List five North American native languages that are spoken in the United States. Is the situation of these languages very different from that of Guaraní in Paraguay?

Paso 2. As you now know from viewing the video segment on the languages of Paraguay, Guaraní has contributed more than any other language to the subjects of flora, fauna, and botanical medicine. Make a list of 10 such words or terms and then share them with the rest of the class. You may consult an encyclopedia or the Internet.

3-3. Bolivia y Paraguay. Bolivia and Paraguay both claim the nickname *El Corazón de América del Sur* (The Heart of South America). Look at a map of South America and, with a classmate, decide which country is right in attributing itself this nickname. Give at least three reasons for your answer.

IV. Class Activities

4-1. **Bolivia and the sea.** Bolivia is a landlocked country. It formally lost its one seacoast possession, the Port of Antofagasta, after being defeated by Chile in the War of the Pacific (*Guerra del Pacífico*) at the end of the nineteenth century. Today, Chile is considering granting Bolivia access to the coast, but Bolivia's position is that such a right must include sovereignty over this access. Because Chile is interested in Bolivia's huge natural gas reserves, it is willing to consider this demand. Consult the Internet to familiarize yourself with the debate surrounding this topic. Then, answer the questions below based on your findings.

1. Do you think Bolivia should have access to the sea? Why or why not?

2. Do you think full sovereignty should be granted along with access?

3. Do you believe Chile should grant Bolivia access in exchange for natural gas?

4-2. **A Paraguayan writer.** Augusto Roa Bastos is a very well-known Paraguayan writer whose short stories and novels "translated" the unique and practically unknown Paraguayan culture to a language that the rest of the world could understand.

Paso 1. Consult the Internet to familiarize yourself with information about Roa Bastos' life and work. Then, prepare a brief report on him to present to the class.

Paso 2. Imagine that Roa Bastos is still alive and, working with the class, compose a letter to him. Each student should prepare a set of five questions about the role of the Guaraní language in Paraguayan society and in Roa Bastos' work. In class, compile the questions and distribute them among groups of three or four. Each group should then compose one paragraph based on two or three related questions.

Chile

INTRODUCTION

This video presents basic information about Chile. You will learn about the country's weather, landscape, cuisine, economy, the way its people speak Spanish, and its writers.

To complete some of the exercises below you will have to watch the video in accordance with the exercise directions. You may choose to view the video segments all at once, individually, and with or without the volume.

USEFUL VOCABULARY

Expresiones

fiesta caballa	*a great party*

Geografía y habitantes

Cordillera de los Andes	*Andean mountains*
Isla de Pascua	*Easter Island*
temperatura cálida	*warm temperature*
costa	*coast, shore*
indígenas	*indigenous people*
mapuches	*indigenous group from the southern part of the country*
aymaras	*indigenous group from the northern part of the country*

Productos y comidas

minas de cobre	*copper mines*
ganado	*cattle*
petróleo	*oil*
vino	*wine*
mariscos	*seafood*
congrio	*conger eel (fish)*

lenguado	*sole fish*
corvina	*corvina (fish)*
choros	*mussels*
manjar(es)	*something exquisite*
pebre	*sauce made of cilantro, onion, lemon, and oil*
locos	*abalones, type of mollusk*
molusco	*mollusk*
pastel de choclo	*corn casserole*
humitas	*corn paste wrapped in corn leaves*
empanada	*meat turnover*

Idiomas y formas de hablar

mapudungu	*language spoken by the Mapuches*
aymara	*language spoken by the Aymaras*
rapa nui	*language spoken by the indigenous people of Easter Island*
quechua	*language spoken by the Incas and their descendants*
guagua	*baby*
porotos	*beans*
palta	*avocado*
pololo/a	*boyfriend/girlfriend*
pichín	*a little bit of something*
copucha	*gossip*
cabros/as	*guys/girls*

Fiestas y celebraciones

Fiesta de la Tirana	*celebration in La Tirana, a town in the north of Chile*
ramadas	*temporary constructions made from branches to celebrate the Chilean national day*
cueca	*Chilean national dance*
salsoteca	*place to dance salsa*

Arte

artesanías	*handicrafts*
objetos de greda	*clay objects*
chanchito de tres patas	*small clay pig with three feet that brings good luck*
mascarón de barco	*figurehead*

I. Before Viewing

1-1. Basic facts about Chile. Consult the Internet and answer the following questions about Chile.

  1. Where is Chile located?

  2. When is Chile's independence day?

  3. List three countries that share a border with Chile.

  4. Name a desert located in Chile.

  5. Name three Chilean writers.

  6. Name two Chilean politicians.

  7. List three Chilean cities.

  8. Describe a historical event that occurred in Chile.

1-2. A map of Chile. Draw a map of Chile and indicate where the **Chiloé Island, Isla de Pascua (*Easter Island*), Andes Mountains**, and **Pacific Ocean** are located.

1-3. Geography in the United States. With a classmate make a list of some **islands, deserts**, and **mountains** located in the United States.

1-4. **Categories.** Research the meaning of the following words and group them according to the categories below.

lenguado	salsoteca	palta
porotos	pastel de choclo	congrio
aymara	disfraces	mapudungu
corvina	ramadas	empanada
cueca	quechua	choros
humitas	rapa nui	

LENGUAS	PESCADOS Y MARISCOS	ACTIVIDADES SOCIALES	OTRAS COMIDAS

1-5. **Comparing food.** Some typical foods from Chile are made out of corn. Can you mention one? What dishes are made out of corn in the United States? Mention two.

II. While Viewing

2-1. **El clima de Chile.** Watch closely the segment, **El clima y el paisaje de Chile**, about weather in the country and complete the following paragraph with information from the video. You may view the segment more than once.

En Chile hay cuatro estaciones: otoño (1) _____________, invierno y (2) _____________.

El desierto de Atacama tiene una temperatura (3) _____________ durante todo el

año y llueve muy poco. En el centro y en el sur el (4) _____________ es más

frío, y cae nieve en las (5) _____________ y en el extremo sur. En el

centro y en el sur el verano tiene (6) _____________ muy agradables y

en el otoño los paisajes toman diferentes (7) _____________. Gracias a sus

montañas, Chile tiene (8) _____________.

2-2. Modos de hablar de los chilenos. Watch the segment, **Modos de hablar de los chilenos,** about the ways people in Chile speak Spanish and determine if the sentences below are true (**Cierto**) or false (**Falso**). Correct the statements that are false.

1. La lengua española no incorporó palabras de las lenguas indígenas de Chile.

❐ **Cierto**   ❐ **Falso**

____

2. El mapudungu fue una de las lenguas indígenas que sobrevivió.

❐ **Cierto**   ❐ **Falso**

____

3. Los mapuches o araucanos son el grupo minoritario más numeroso de Chile.

❐ **Cierto**   ❐ **Falso**

____

4. El aymara es una lengua indígena que se habla en el sur de Chile.

❐ **Cierto**   ❐ **Falso**

____

5. El rapa nui es una lengua indígena que se habla en la Isla de Pascua.

❐ **Cierto**   ❐ **Falso**

____

6. El vocabulario de los chilenos tiene palabras del quechua.

❐ **Cierto**   ❐ **Falso**

____

7. *Choclo, guagua* y *poroto* son palabras que tienen su origen en el mapudungu.

❐ **Cierto**   ❐ **Falso**

____

8. *Pololos* y *pichín* son palabras que tienen su origen en el quechua.

❏ **Cierto**　　　❏ **Falso**

____

9. Las fiestas caballas en Chile son muy buenas.

❏ **Cierto**　　　❏ **Falso**

____

10. La palabra *palta* viene del rapa nui.

❏ **Cierto**　　　❏ **Falso**

____

2-3. **La comida.** Watch the segment on **La comida de Chile**.

Paso 1. With a classmate, make a list of fish and shellfish that Chilean people eat and another list with the fish and shellfish that American people eat. You can consult the Internet to find more information.

Paso 2. Is there any fish or shellfish that Chilean people eat, but American people do not or vice versa? Which ones? What do you think are the reasons for these dietary differences?

2-4. **Chilean writers.** Watch the segment, **Chile: tierra de poetas**, about Chilean poets and describe Pablo Neruda's house shown in the video.

III. After Viewing

3-1. Una receta chilena. You have learned about foods and dishes in the Chilean diet. Using the Internet, find a Chilean recipe to share with the class. Write the ingredients and how it is prepared. Do you think you would like this dish? Why or why not?

3-2. Your opinion. Based on what you have learned about Chile, you can now provide your opinions about the country's economy, people, celebrations and customs. Have you seen aspects of Chilean life that differ from your own? In groups of four discuss these differences. Then describe some similarities and differences between Chile and your country. Consider the following topics in your analysis.

	Chile	My country:______________
El clima		
El paisaje		
La economía		
Las lenguas		
Las celebraciones		
Las compras		
La vida nocturna		

3-3. Un poema. During your investigation about Chile and in the video you have learned about different Chilean poets like Pablo Neruda, Gabriela Mistral, and Nicanor Parra. Read a poem written by one of these authors and answer the following questions: What is the subject of the poem? What does it describe? Is it a sad or a happy poem? What is the poem's message?

4-1. A Chilean writer in the United States. Isabel Allende is a Chilean writer who lives in the United States. You are probably familiar with some of her books, like *The House of the Spirits* or *Of Love and Shadows*. You may also have seen the movies based on these books.

Paso 1. Visit a Web page about the author and familiarize yourself with the information you find. Prepare a brief report to present to the class.

Paso 2. Role play. Isabel Allende is visiting your class and will be taking questions from the audience. Select a member of the class to act as Allende; the rest of the class will act as the audience. Prepare two to three questions you would like to ask the author.

Colombia

INTRODUCTION

This video presents basic information about Colombia, a country in South America with many interesting places to visit. Get ready to enjoy the trip!

USEFUL VOCABULARY

patria	*homeland*	aire libre	*outdoors*
orfebrería	*goldsmithing, silversmithing*	rodeada	*surrounded*
		eje	*axis*

I. Before Viewing

1-1. Datos sobre Colombia. What do you know about Colombia? Write down five words to describe this country and then, with a partner, take turns explaining why you chose the words.

1-2. Más sobre Colombia. Based on your knowledge of Colombia circle the answers below you believe are correct.

1. Geográficamente, Colombia es:

   a. la puerta de entrada a Suramérica

   b. un país al sur de Suramérica

   c. una isla

2. Este país es rico en:
   a. diamantes
   b. café
   c. maíz

3. Colombia:
   a. tiene dos costas
   b. no tiene mar
   c. tiene muy poca agua

4. Un héroe nacional de Colombia es:
   a. George Washington
   b. Francisco Madero
   c. Simón Bolívar

5. La capital es:
   a. Caracas
   b. Lima
   c. Santafé de Bogotá

6. La capital está en:
   a. una sabana
   b. un valle
   c. el mar

7. En Colombia hay muchos:
   a. parques
   b. trenes
   c. museos

II. While Viewing

2-1. **¿Cierto o falso?** Based on the information in the video, indicate whether the following sentences are true (**Cierto**) or false (**Falso**). Correct any false statements.

1. Colombia es un brazo de Suramérica.

❏ Cierto   ❏ Falso

____

2. La capital de Colombia es Barranquilla.

❏ Cierto   ❏ Falso

____

3. Éste es un país de muy poca variedad geográfica.

❏ Cierto   ❏ Falso

____

4. Dos ríos importantes son el Magdalena y el Caribe.

❏ Cierto   ❏ Falso

____

5. En la capital hay muchos museos y actividades culturales.

❏ Cierto   ❏ Falso

____

6. Un museo con una colección importante es el Museo del Oro.

❏ Cierto   ❏ Falso

____

7. En la capital no hay ningún museo histórico.

   ❏ **Cierto**   ❏ **Falso**

   ____

8. Otro lugar para visitar en Colombia es la selva.

   ❏ **Cierto**   ❏ **Falso**

   ____

9. En Colombia hay un Parque del Café.

   ❏ **Cierto**   ❏ **Falso**

   ____

10. Cartagena de Indias es una ciudad histórica.

    ❏ **Cierto**   ❏ **Falso**

    ____

2-2. **Palabras clave.** In the table below write down six key words from the video. Then, with a classmate, take turns asking questions or giving clues to help each other guess the words you have chosen.

III. After Viewing

3-1. Un viaje a Colombia. Imagine that, during International Week at your university, one of the prizes was a trip to Colombia and you won! With a partner talk about what you are going to do while in Colombia. Use the following questions as a guide:

1. ¿Cuándo y cómo vas a llegar a Colombia?

2. ¿Qué tipo de ropa vas a llevar? ¿Por qué?

3. ¿Cuáles son algunas de las actividades culturales que vas a hacer cuando estés en la ciudad?

4. ¿Qué tipo de comida vas a probar? ¿Por qué?

5. ¿Qué vas a decirle a tu familia sobre Colombia a tu regreso?

3-2. ¡Mi puente en Colombia! In Colombia most holidays are celebrated by law on Mondays with the exception of some religious and national holidays that are observed on their actual dates. These long weekends are known as **puentes**, which means "bridges." Imagine that you and two of your classmates are studying Spanish in Colombia and for the last **puente**, each of you visited a different place in the city or in the country. After the long weekend the three of you get together to compare notes, to talk about the places you visited, the people you met, and, of course, your favorite food during your trip. Write a summary about what the members of your group did and share it with the class.

3-3. ¡Veo, veo! (*I spy!*) Imagine that you and your friends were the videographers for the video you just saw. Together, play the popular game **¡Veo, veo!** and describe what you saw while filming in Colombia. Who can see and remember the most? As you play, try to incorporate vocabulary you have learned in the video.

3-4. Comparaciones. Compare and contrast your country with Colombia. Use the questions below as a guide and compare the different items from the list that follows: comida, geografía, museos, educación, ríos, y costas.

1. ¿En qué aspectos son similares?

2. ¿En qué se diferencian?

4-1. **Más sobre Colombia I.** Consult the Internet for information about **one** of the following topics regarding your country: government, geography, food, culture, tourism, national heroes. Then, do the same for Colombia and look for similarities and differences between the two countries. Present your findings to the class.

4-2. **Más sobre Colombia II.** Consult the Internet for more information about one of the topics mentioned in the video: the Gold Museum, Monserrate, el Parque del Café, or Cartagena de Indias, for example. Present your findings to the class and explain why you are interested in that topic.

4-3. **¿Conoces Colombia?** Using what you wrote about Colombia at the beginning of this video segment (Activity 1-1) report to your classmates if the ideas you had about this country were accurate. Then tell what you have learned about Colombia and if and how your opinion has changed.

Costa Rica

INTRODUCTION

The video you are about to view presents basic information on Costa Rica, a small country in Central America. You will learn information about Costa Rica's geography, capital, climate, and tourist attractions.

To complete some of the exercises below you will need to view the video as directed: all at once, individually, and with or without the volume.

USEFUL VOCABULARY

Expresiones

¡Pura vida!	*Life is good!*
ticos	*Costa Ricans*

Una visita a San José

pieza	*piece*
joya	*jewel*

La naturaleza y el clima

naturaleza	*nature*
abundante	*abundant*
cordillera	*mountain range*
antigua	*old*

El turismo

ola	*wave*
balsa	*boat*
época	*time*
sendero	*path*

I. Before Viewing

1-1. Información. What do you know about *ecoturism* in Costa Rica?

Watch the video segment **Turismo en Costa Rica** without sound and describe what you see. Your description should answer the following questions: Who is surfing at the beach? What are the people doing before going rafting? What must one wear when going rafting? Why are there suspension bridges in the forest?

1-2. Viaje de aventura.

Paso 1. List the types of things you would **take with you** and the things you would **do** on an adventure trip.

Paso 2. With a group of classmates, compare the information you have gathered. Then plan a trip to a specific place: a mountain, a beach, or a volcano, for example. Present your ideal trip to the class.

1-3. Preguntas personales.

Paso 1. Answer the following questions before watching the video.

a. Have you ever been to a rain forest? Where? What did you do there?

b. Have you ever seen an active volcano? Where? What was it like?

Paso 2. Now share your answers with the rest of the class and see how many of your classmates have visited these amazing places.

II. While Viewing

2-1. Completar. Watch the segment, **Una visita a San José,** and complete the following sentences based on what you see and hear in the video.

Los costarricenses son personas muy tranquilas, educadas y (1) ___________________.

San José es la (2) ________________ de Costa Rica y es donde vive la mayor

parte de los (3) ________________. Sus principales (4) ________________ están

llenas de gente que camina y va de (5) ________________ a las tiendas. Un paseo

con la (6) ________________ o amigos por la famosa Plaza de la Cultura, es una

buena forma de (7) ________________.

2-2. Cierto o falso. ¿Cuánto sabes de Costa Rica? Watch the video once again. Determine if the following statements are true (**Cierto**) or false (**Falso**) based on your knowledge of Costa Rica, its culture and history, and what you have seen and heard in the video. Correct any false statements.

1. Costa Rica es un país pequeño ubicado en América del Sur.

   ❏ **Cierto**   ❏ **Falso**

   ____

2. La población de Costa Rica es de aproximadamente 4 millones de habitantes.

   ❏ **Cierto**   ❏ **Falso**

   ____

3. Los costarricenses son de descendencia española.

   ❏ **Cierto**   ❏ **Falso**

   ____

4. Los **ticos** no están muy conscientes sobre la protección de los bosques y animales.

   ❏ **Cierto**   ❏ **Falso**

   ____

5. Existen cinco cordilleras en Costa Rica.

   ❏ **Cierto**   ❏ **Falso**

   ____

6. La Plaza de la Cultura es un lugar ideal para ir de compras y visitar con la familia.

   ❏ **Cierto**   ❏ **Falso**

   ____

7. El Teatro Nacional es una joya nacional y se construyó hace 50 años.

   ❏ **Cierto**   ❏ **Falso**

   ____

8. Más de 2 millones de turistas visitan Costa Rica al año.

❒ **Cierto**   ❒ **Falso**

____

9. La cultura afrocaribeña se encuentra en la provincia de Limón.

❒ **Cierto**   ❒ **Falso**

____

10. Un 25% del territorio nacional está protegido por el gobierno de Costa Rica.

❒ **Cierto**   ❒ **Falso**

____

2-3. **Ordenar.** Watch **Una visita a San José** and put the following statements in the correct order according to what you see and hear in this segment of the video.

_______ **a.** El Museo de Oro se encuentra a unos pasos de la Plaza de la Cultura.

_______ **b.** Podemos encontrar zapatos, ropa, artesanía y muchas cosas más.

_______ **c.** Un paseo con la familia o amigos es una buena forma de pasar el rato.

_______ **d.** El Teatro Nacional es considerado una "joya nacional".

_______ **e.** El turista disfruta de la gran variedad de artículos a la venta.

2-4. **El paisaje.** As you watch the video segment **El turismo en Costa Rica,** place a check mark beside the things you see.

_______ **1.** playas

_______ **2.** un río

_______ **3.** una laguna

_______ **4.** unos árboles

_______ **5.** un volcán

_______ **6.** unos peces

III. After Viewing

3-1. Una entrevista. Work with a classmate and ask each other the following questions. Then, compare your answers.

1. ¿Te gusta cuidar y conservar la naturaleza? ¿Por qué es importante hacerlo?

2. ¿Qué deportes al aire libre te gusta practicar?

3. ¿Qué actividades te gusta hacer con tus amigos cuando van a la playa?

4. ¿En tu opinión cuál sería un lugar ideal para pasar unas buenas vacaciones en Costa Rica? ¿Por qué escogiste ese lugar?

3-2. Un viaje increíble. Imagine you are visiting Costa Rica. After visiting the rain forest, volcanoes, and beaches, you want to convince your best friend to come and join you. Write a brief letter in Spanish to that friend about your experience and try to convince him/her to visit Costa Rica.

IV. Class Activities

4-1. Presentación. With a classmate, prepare a presentation about one of the following sports/hobbies to present to the class.

Surfing   Water Rafting   Hiking

Be sure to mention the following: What kind of equipment is necessary to use and/or wear? Where is a good place to practice this sport? What makes this kind of sport so popular?

Cuba

INTRODUCTION

This video presents basic information about Cuba, one of the many countries where Spanish is spoken. You will learn information about Cuba's geography, climate, ecology, history, and economy. We hope you gain a new perspective about this island that lies only 90 miles from the United States.

In order to do some of the following activities, you will need to view the video as directed: first view it without the volume, view it again with the volume, and then view individual segments.

USEFUL VOCABULARY

Arquitectura:

fortaleza	*fortress*
iglesia	*church*

Fauna:

caracol	*shell*	nido	*nest*
hembra	*female animal*	polimitas	*snails*
macho	*male animal*	zunzún	*bee hummingbird*
mariposa	*butterfly*		

Geografía:

cadenas montañosas	*mountain ranges*
llano	*plain*

Historia:

cacique	*indian chief*	siglo	*century*
pulimentar	*to gloss or polish*	tallar	*to cut or chop*

Tabaco:

aspirar	*to breathe in*	masticar	*chew*
capote	*top leaf*	torcer	*to twist or roll*
girar	*to turn round*	tripa	*filler*

I. Before Viewing

1-1. Do you know Cuba? What basic information do you already know about Cuba?

Paso 1. List three things that immediately come to mind when someone mentions Cuba. Compare your list with those of your classmates. Find one or two students who have the same things on their list as you. Working together, write a brief paragraph with as much information as possible regarding the topic(s) you have in common.

Paso 2. Many times we don't give ourselves credit for knowing a lot about another country when, in fact, due to popular culture in movies, music, and other forums, we have more knowledge than we realized. See how many of these places, persons, or things related to Cuba you can match correctly:

1. _____ Desi Arnaz
2. _____ Guantánamo
3. _____ zunzún
4. _____ mambo
5. _____ José Martí
6. _____ El Morro
7. _____ yuca
8. _____ Buena Vista Social Club
9. _____ Orlando Hernández
10. _____ guayaba

a. a root and very popular food
b. a dance
c. a group of older singers from Cuba
d. a fruit
e. a bandleader married to Lucille Ball
f. a city and American base
g. a bee hummingbird
h. a famous writer and Cuban hero
i. a famous fortress
j. a baseball pitcher in the major leagues

Paso 3. There are many Cubans in the United States who have impacted our society. Choose a Cuban with whom you are familiar (whether it's a friend or a famous person) and write a brief paragraph about him or her and what you personally have learned about the country and its people from that individual. If you need suggestions your instructor will have a list of names for you to consult.

1-2. Vocabulario activo. Find and circle the vocabulary words that are listed below. To make this activity more challenging, work in pairs and time yourselves. See who can find all 15 words fastest.

```
G  S  S  R  I  C  S  D  N  M  E  Q  O  I  L
H  J  M  R  V  S  A  T  A  P  M  C  W  G  L
G  O  Y  A  C  Y  Ñ  C  O  N  A  O  A  L  E
D  O  M  I  N  Ó  A  E  I  B  Z  S  X  E  U
Z  K  R  K  U  F  T  Y  A  Q  O  Ó  V  S  C
W  K  I  A  Y  A  N  T  X  P  U  U  N  I  C
P  C  A  R  A  C  O  L  I  P  Y  E  E  A  A
N  A  P  D  F  S  M  R  H  X  C  S  H  O  E
A  R  B  M  E  H  A  S  Z  H  V  L  Q  A  P
S  D  H  L  R  M  I  S  A  D  A  L  L  Z  P
R  O  V  U  A  C  J  V  O  C  W  A  K  C  I
Z  R  P  B  L  N  E  L  U  N  M  N  N  V  J
Q  S  P  P  L  T  U  E  U  M  Í  O  W  W  D
G  J  C  K  A  W  M  E  E  Y  I  A  M  S  Z
P  W  G  Q  T  I  Z  I  K  B  B  S  T  O  Z
```

cacique	dominó	montañas
caracol	hembra	poeta
cayo	iglesia	tabaco
chaveta	llano	taínos
danzón	mariposa	tallar

II. While Viewing

2-1. Cierto o falso. While watching the video, pay special attention to the facts and figures provided. Determine if the following statements are true (**Cierto**) or false (**Falso**) according to your observations. Correct any false statements.

	Cierto	**Falso**
1. Cuba es una isla pequeña situada en el mar caribe.	❐	❐
2. La Isla de la Juventud se llamaba Isla de Pinos.	❐	❐

<table>
<tr><td></td><td></td><td>**Cierto**</td><td>**Falso**</td></tr>
<tr><td>**3.**</td><td>Cuba es un país llano con tres cadenas montañosas.</td><td>❒</td><td>❒</td></tr>
<tr><td>**4.**</td><td>El zunzún se encuentra en muchos países tropicales.</td><td>❒</td><td>❒</td></tr>
<tr><td>**5.**</td><td>En Cuba hay más de 7.000 especies de plantas y animales.</td><td>❒</td><td>❒</td></tr>
<tr><td>**6.**</td><td>Había tres grupos de indígenas en Cuba cuando llegaron los españoles.</td><td>❒</td><td>❒</td></tr>
<tr><td>**7.**</td><td>Un cacique es un miembro del ejército español.</td><td>❒</td><td>❒</td></tr>
<tr><td>**8.**</td><td>José Martí es un héroe nacional en Cuba.</td><td>❒</td><td>❒</td></tr>
<tr><td>**9.**</td><td>Santiago de Cuba es la capital del país.</td><td>❒</td><td>❒</td></tr>
<tr><td>**10.**</td><td>Los españoles trajeron el tabaco a Cuba.</td><td>❒</td><td>❒</td></tr>
</table>

2-2. Reconociendo datos.

Paso 1. Watch the entire video with the volume turned off. Then, write down four topics you can recall and provide a few details about each.

Paso 2. Working with a classmate, compare the topics each of you were able to recall. Choose one of the topics and, together, consult the Internet to find out more about it. Then write a brief report on your findings and present it to the class.

2-3. El tabaco. Cuban cigars are famous the world over. Watch the video segment about tobacco and the making of cigars and then put the following sentences in sequential order based on what you observed.

1. _________________________   **A.** Los tabacos son torcidos a mano.

2. _________________________   **B.** Los tabacos se ponen en un molde de madera.

3. _________________________   **C.** Los indios masticaban las hojas de una planta.

4. _________________________   **D.** La chaveta se usa para darle forma al tabaco.

5. _________________________   **E.** Los indios quemaban la planta y aspiraban el humo.

6. _________________________   **F.** Cada tabaquero tiene su secreto de cómo hacer un buen tabaco.

III. After Viewing

3-1. Medios de transporte en Cuba. We can see from the video that Cuban cars are not of the latest model. Consult the Internet to find out what other modes of transportation Cubans use.

1. ¿Qué es un camello?

2. ¿Cuál es la diferencia entre un "cocotaxi" y un "bicitaxi"?

3. ¿Cómo es el transporte en Cuba para los cubanos? Explica.

4. Lee sobre los "autos antiguos" en Cuba y da tu opinión sobre los cubanos que mantienen estos autos.

4-1. Pop Culture and Poetry. Many musicians have taken words from poetry and re-written them as song lyrics. Working in groups of three or four find out what the song *Guantanamera* and José Martí's poem *Versos sencillos* have in common. Consult the Internet to find information about this fusion of pop culture and poetry and report back to the class.

- ¿Quién escribió la canción *Guantanamera*?
- ¿Quién escribió la música para esta canción?
- ¿Qué significa *Guantanamera*?
- ¿Qué tiene en común esta canción con *Versos sencillos* de Martí?
- ¿Quién(es) de tu grupo conoce(n) la canción *Guantanamera*?

Expliquen el significado de las letras de la canción.

4-2. Cubanos famosos en los EE.UU. There are many famous Cubans now living in the United States. With a partner, choose someone from Cuba with whom you are familiar, or about whom you would like to know more, and create a PowerPoint presentation highlighting that individual. You may consult the Internet to gather as much information as possible. Use the following questions as a guide when preparing your presentation:

1. ¿Dónde nació él o ella? ¿En Cuba o en EE.UU.?
2. ¿Dónde vive ahora?
3. ¿Cuándo vino a los EE.UU.?
4. ¿Cuál es su profesión actual?
5. ¿Cómo es su personalidad?
6. ¿Cómo ha contribuido esta persona a la sociedad de los EE.UU.?
7. ¿Te gustaría conocer a esta persona?
8. ¿Qué aprendiste al leer sobre este personaje?

Ecuador

INTRODUCTION

This video presents basic information about Ecuador, one of the Latin American countries where Spanish is spoken. You will learn about Ecuador's population, geography, nature, history, art, and cuisine. We hope you enjoy this presentation.

In order to do some of the exercises below, you will need to view the video as directed: view all at once, in individual segments, or without the volume.

USEFUL VOCABULARY

Expresiones

¡Como para chuparse los dedos!	*Finger licking good!*

Introducción

limita	*it borders*	zona lluviosa	*rainy area*
diversidad	*diversity*	zona seca	*dry area*

La población de Ecuador

conviven	*cohabit*	pueblos	*towns*
debido	*due to*	multicultural	*multicultural*
crecer	*to grow*	nacionalidad	*nationality*
migración	*migration*	indígena	*indigenous*

La geografía de Ecuador

llanura	*plain*	cordillera	*mountain range*
colina	*hill*	selva	*jungle*
playa	*beach*	volcán	*volcano*

La naturaleza de Ecuador

pájaro	*bird*	caminata	*hiking*
mariposa	*butterfly*	cabalgata	*horse riding*
reptil	*reptile*	buceo	*scuba diving*
biodiversidad	*biodiversity*	canotaje	*canoeing*
fogata	*bonfire/campfire*		

El pasado histórico de Ecuador

sociedad aborígen	*aborigenous society*	creencia	*belief*
someter	*to subject*	durar	*to last*

La economía de Ecuador

empresario	*entrepreneur/ business person*	producción artesanal	*handmade production*
intercambio	*exchange*	plata	*silver*
industria maderera	*wood industry/timber*	oro	*gold*
centro financiero	*financial center*	petróleo	*petroleum, oil*

La cocina ecuatoriana

porotos	*beans*	empanada	*turnover*
gusto	*taste*	yuca	*manioc*
maíz	*corn*	plato típico	*typical dish*

Las Islas Galápagos

piqueros de patas rojas	*redfooted boobies*	túnel de lava	*lava tunnel*
fauna	*fauna*	buceo	*snorkling*
archipiélago	*archipelago*	paraíso	*paradise*
arena	*sand*	tortuga	*tortoise*

I. Before Viewing

1-1. **¿Qué sabes sobre Ecuador?** Complete the following sentences with the correct information:

    1. La religión principal de Ecuador es _______________________________.

    2. En Ecuador se habla español y _______________________________.

    3. La moneda oficial de Ecuador es el _______________________________.

    4. Unas islas famosas de Ecuador son _______________________________.

    5. El océano que está al oeste del Ecuador se llama _______________________________.

II. While Viewing

2-1. A completar. Watch the video about Ecuador and fill the blanks below with the correct information.

1. Ecuador está situado al _________________ de América del Sur.

2. El idioma oficial del país es el _____________________________.

3. El territorio ecuatoriano está formado por llanuras, _________________,

   playas, sierras, _______________, islas y selvas.

4. Ecuador es uno de los países donde está concentrada la mayor

   _______________ del planeta.

2-2. A circular. Complete the statements below with the correct response.

1. La cordillera de los Andes divide a Ecuador en . . .

   a. dos regiones.   **b.** tres regiones.   **c.** cuatro regiones.

2. En Ecuador hay una gran variedad de lenguas indígenas, de las cuales la más hablada es . . .

   a. el quichua.   **b.** el shuara.   **c.** el navajo.

3. Las Islas Galápagos se componen de:

   a. 13 islas principales.   **b.** 20 islas principales.   **c.** 5 islas principales.

4. El lugar de asiento del imperio Inca fue . . .

   a. la región de la costa.   **b.** el sur de Chile.   **c.** la región de los Andes y de la costa de Ecuador.

5. El centro económico del país es . . .

   a. Cuenca.   **b.** Guayaquil.   **c.** Quito.

2-3. **¿Cierto o falso?** Indicate if the following sentences are true **(Cierto)** or false **(Falso)**.

	Cierto	Falso
1. Ecuador no tiene variaciones significativas en su clima.	❏	❏
2. Ecuador tiene una población multicultural.	❏	❏
3. El origen de las islas Galápagos es volcánico.	❏	❏
4. El petróleo es la fuente principal de ingresos para el país.	❏	❏
5. No existe tierra volcánica en ninguna de las Islas Galápagos.	❏	❏

2-4. **En parejas.** With a partner, write five sentences describing what you now know about Ecuador. Use words from the list below if necessary.

indígenas	fauna	pájaros	artesanía
mariposas	este	petróleo	árboles
amazonía	Andes	norte	producto principal
sur	pueblos	montañas	

III. After Viewing

3-1. **A contestar.** Answer the following questions with complete sentences based on the information from the video.

1. ¿Qué son y dónde están situados el Cayambe, el Chimborazo y el Cotopaxi?

2. ¿Qué tipo de clima tienen las Islas Galápagos?

3. ¿Cuántos habitantes hay en Ecuador?

4. ¿En cuántas regiones se divide el país?

3-2. A corregir. Read the following sentences and then rewrite them correcting the false information.

1. La sierra tiene importantes praderas y volcanes.

2. El imperio de los Incas existió después de la llegada de los españoles.

3. Cuenca, la capital, es el centro político y financiero del país.

4. La comida del indígena ecuatoriano está basada en tres productos: tomate, pepinos y porotos.

5. Las Islas Galápagos se encuentran a casi tres mil kilómetros de distancia del continente.

3-3. Una visita a Ecuador. Write a paragraph describing where in Ecuador you would like to visit and why.

España

INTRODUCTION

This video presents basic information about Spain. You will learn about Spain's geography, economy, art, traditions, typical cuisine, and everyday life. We hope you enjoy this presentation.

In order to do some of the exercises below, you will need to view the video as directed: all at once, by individual segments, or without the volume.

USEFUL VOCABULARY

Expresiones

¡Buen provecho!	*Enjoy your meal!*
en fin	*Finally, so*

Productos y comidas

oliva, aceituna	*olive*	aceite	*oil*
olivo	*olive tree*	cuero	*leather*
girasol	*sunflower*		

Idiomas

catalán	*Catalan*
vasco/euskera	*Basque*
Gallego	*Galician*

Fiestas y tradiciones

desfiles	*parades*
San Fermín	*San Fermin Celebration (running of the bulls)*
Feria de Sevilla	*Seville's Fair (music and dance celebration)*
Procesiones de Semana Santa	*Fire Celebrations*
Fallas de Valencia	*Easter Processions*

jotas	country folk dances		
guitarra	guitar		
flauta	flute		
gaita	bagpipe		
celta	celtic		
mercadillo	open-air market		

Arte

| hispano-árabe | Spanish-Arab | arco | arch |
| mezquita | mosque | | |

I. Before Viewing

1-1. Los hechos. What basic information do you already know about Spain?

Paso 1. Complete the chart below with information you know about Spain, its culture, and its people. Do you know any famous Spanish writers, actors, or musicians? How many cities can you name? Who is the president of Spain? Can you name a famous Spanish artist?

	España
Escritor/a	
Músico/a	
Cantante	
Artista	
Político/a	
Celebración	
Ciudad	
Comida o producto típico	

Paso 2. Work in groups to compare the information you have gathered about Spain with information about your own country. Then, with a classmate, write a brief paragraph in which you compare aspects of the two countries, for example, famous people, geography, or languages. Share your findings on these similarities and differences with the class.

1-2. Ensalada de palabras.

Paso 1. With your partner, group the following words into the following three themes: **comidas, fiestas y celebraciones** and **lugares y monumentos**.

arco	aceite	festejar	mezquita	tambores	vino	columna
público	catedral	sala	frutas	desfile	girasol	
tapa	mariscos	procesión	edificio	música		

Paso 2. Make sure you know the meanings of these words. You may use your dictionary if necessary. In groups, decide which of these words are related to your culture or to a culture in your country. For example, is there a typical meal that contains olives in American cuisine? Is there a mosque nearby or in your town? Select five of these topics and present information on them to the class.

II. While Viewing

2-1. Trivia. ¿Qué sabes sobre España? Watch the first five minutes of the video again. Determine if the following statements are true (**Cierto**) or false (**Falso**) based on your knowledge about Spain, its culture and history, and what you see and hear in the video. Correct any false statements.

1. España es una isla en el sur de Europa.

   ❏ **Cierto**   ❏ **Falso**

   ____

2. Las Islas Canarias están en el Océano Atlántico, junto a África, pero son parte de España.

   ❏ **Cierto**   ❏ **Falso**

   ____

3. España es un país muy pequeño, con menos de 10 millones de habitantes.

   ❏ **Cierto**   ❏ **Falso**

   ____

4. La moneda nacional es el euro desde el año 2002.

   ❏ **Cierto**   ❏ **Falso**

   ____

5. En España se produce aceite de maní, principalmente.

❑ **Cierto**   ❑ **Falso**

____

6. Portugal está al oeste de España. Los dos países juntos forman la Península Ibérica.

❑ **Cierto**   ❑ **Falso**

____

7. En todas las regiones de España el clima es caluroso y los paisajes son tropicales.

❑ **Cierto**   ❑ **Falso**

____

8. Un plato típico de España son los tamales.

❑ **Cierto**   ❑ **Falso**

____

9. En España no hay montañas, sólo hay campos y llanuras.

❑ **Cierto**   ❑ **Falso**

____

10. En España se habla el español y las lenguas indígenas, como el quechua y el gallego.

❑ **Cierto**   ❑ **Falso**

____

2-2. **La comida.** Watch the segment of a restaurant where **tapas** are displayed at the bar counter. Complete the following paragraph based on what you see and hear in the video. Select from the following list of words.

¡Buen provecho!	aire libre	pollo
nos reunimos	sabrosas	
mariscos	verduras	

Las comidas típicas españolas son muy (1) _____________. Aunque uno de los platos más típicos es la paella, hecha de arroz, (2) _____________, (3) _____________ y (4) _____________, las tapas también son muy populares. En este bar vemos unas tapas, o aperitivos. Los españoles comemos las tapas cuando (5) _____________ con amigos o con la familia, para tomar una cerveza en un bar o en una terraza al (6) _____________. Cuando un español te desea una buena comida, dice (7): "_____________".

III. After Viewing

3-1. Horario de vacaciones.

Paso 1. With a classmate, create a schedule for a day trip to a Spanish city. Choose the city in which you plan to stay and the activities you will do. Include times of day, types of transportation, meals, leisure activities, at least one cultural site, and an evening activity.

	Lugar	Actividad
Mañana		
Tarde		
Noche		

Paso 2. Now discuss your schedule with two other pairs of students. Decide what type of tourists you are based on the selection of your activities: Adventurous (**aventurero/a**)? Classy (**con clase**)? Sophisticated (**sofisticado/a**)? Describe the other groups' travel style as well. Use verbs like **gustar, molestar, importar, querer**, and **desear**.

3-2. La comida. What do you know about Spanish **tapas**? There is no specific recipe or rule on how to make a **tapa**. Look at the images in the video segment on **tapas** and write an e-mail to a friend telling him or her how **tapas** are made, and then create your own with the foods you enjoy! You can try to create the best "**tapa estadounidense**," using ingredients typical of your culture. What would you put in your **tapa** and what seasonings would you use?

3-3. Una entrevista. With a classmate, imagine you are interviewing a Spaniard whose job is related to something you saw in this video. Some examples might be a vendor at a street market, a wine maker, an artist, a cook, an athlete, or a fisherman.

Paso 1. First, make a list of questions you would ask the person in relation to his or her job or activity.

Paso 2. Now create a role-play in which one person is the interviewer and the other is the interviewee. Present your dialogue to the class. Be sure to include some of the information you have seen or heard in the video.

3-4. **Una noche inolvidable.** View the video segment on dance and music in which a few couples dance and guitar players perform. In groups answer the following questions and then discuss your answers.

1. ¿Qué hora del día es?

2. ¿Qué crees que están celebrando?

3. ¿Crees que es una celebración formal/religiosa/informal/de vecinos?

4. ¿Cómo son las personas que bailan? ¿Crees que se conocen?

5. ¿Cuál crees que es la relación entre la joven y el hombre de pelo blanco?

6. ¿Qué tipo de ropa llevan las mujeres? ¿Es ropa moderna? ¿Festiva? ¿Tradicional?

IV. Class Activities

4-1. **Un personaje famoso en EE.UU.** Work in groups of three or four and research a famous Spaniard whose life was, or still is, connected to the United States, either by his/her impact on American culture or history or American culture's influence on that person. For example, Federico García Lorca wrote one of his most famous poetry collections after visiting the United States, many actors and actresses have had an American debut after years of fame in Spain, and famous Spanish scientists have worked in American research institutions. Present the most important aspects of your research to your classmates.

Guatemala

INTRODUCTION

You are going to view a video about Guatemala, a Central American country where Spanish is spoken. You will learn about Guatemala's geography, climate, and cities. In addition, you will learn about the historical presence of the Mayans as well as the legacy left behind by the Spanish during colonial times.

USEFUL VOCABULARY

altiplanicies	*highlands*
antigüeño	*a person from Antigua Guatemala*
cadena de volcanes	*a mountain range with volcanoes*
calles empedradas	*cobblestone streets*
terremoto	*earthquake*
K'iche'	*indigenous group*
Kaqchikel	*indigenous group*
Mam	*indigenous group*
Q'eqchi'	*indigenous group*
juego de pelota	*ball game, as practiced by Mesoamerican cultures*
ladino	*term used in Guatemala to refer to Mestizos and persons of European descent or, in general, to the nonindigenous population*
Mesoamérica	*A term archeologists use to refer to a region that includes southwestern Mexico, Guatemala, Belize, and the eastern portion of Honduras and El Salvador*
ofrendas	*religious offerings*
templos reconstruidos	*rebuilt temples*
tierras bajas	*low lands*
valle de la Ermita	*Ermita Valley*
vestirse de gala	*to dress up*

1-1. **¿Qué sabes sobre Guatemala?** Discuss with a classmate what you know and what you would like to know about Guatemala. Make two lists based on each of these categories. Then, compare your lists with another group's. Choose the three subjects that interest you the most and consult the Internet to gather information. Present your findings to the rest of the class.

1-2. **Vocabulario.** Working in small groups, find out the meanings of the following words that relate to the country and culture of Guatemala. How would you categorize these words? Choose appropriate categories by which you can group them, for example, language, religion, or architecture, and then compare your categories and lists with those of your classmates.

agricultura	costumbres	español	selva
antepasados	creencias	maíz	templado
bosques	cultura	ofrendas	tropical
colonial	herencia	ritual	volcanes
conquista	indígena	ruinas	maya

II. While Viewing

2-1. **¡A completar!** As you watch the video, complete the paragraphs below with logical words or phrases based on what you see and hear.

El clima de Guatemala es húmedo y (1) _____________. Tiene límite con cuatro países; dos de ellos son (2) _____________ y (3) _____________. La población de Guatemala es diferente de la de otros países de Centroamérica porque tiene una importante herencia (4) _____________. Las ruinas de (5) _____________, en el Petén, son una muestra de esta herencia. Ahora, los descendientes de esta civilización tienen que luchar para mantener su cultura; una persona importante en esta lucha es la activista (6) _____________, quien ganó el premio Nóbel de la Paz en 1992.

Los españoles llegaron a Guatemala en el año (7) _____________ y trajeron sus propias costumbres, su religión y su idioma. Una ciudad importante durante la época colonial fue (8) _____________, que fue la capital del país por muchos años. Esta ciudad es muy interesante para los turistas porque tiene muchos atractivos, como sus (9) _____________, las ruinas de las (10) _____________ y la arquitectura (11) _____________. A finales del siglo dieciocho, la capital se trasladó al valle de la Ermita, y ahora la Ciudad de Guatemala tiene más de (12) _____________ de habitantes y es el centro de expansión y desarrollo económico del país.

2-2. **Más hechos.** As you watch the video, complete the following questions by selecting the appropriate statement.

1. Guatemala limita al suroeste con . . .

   a. México. **c.** Honduras.

   b. El Salvador. **d.** Belice.

2. Guatemala tiene 180 millas de costas en el . . .

   a. Océano Pacífico. **c.** Mar Caribe.

   b. Océano Atlántico. **d.** Golfo de México.

3. En Guatemala, la zona más productiva para la agricultura está en . . .

   a. las selvas húmedas subtropicales del Petén.

   b. la región entre los volcanes y las costas del Océano Pacífico.

   c. las montañas en el centro del país.

   d. la región oeste del país.

4. La agricultura representa el _______ de la economía del país.

   a. 15% **c.** 30%

   b. 25% **d.** 35%

5. La población de Guatemala está compuesta de . . .

   a. indígenas y mestizos. **c.** indígenas y europeos.

   b. indígenas y españoles. **d.** indígenas y ladinos.

6. Las ruinas de la época maya demuestran conocimientos . . .

   a. de la astronomía.

   b. de las matemáticas.

   c. de la organización de de calendarios.

   d. *all of the above.*

7. Los españoles llegaron a Guatemala en . . .

   a. el siglo dieciséis. **c.** el siglo diecisiete.

   b. el siglo quince. **d.** el siglo catorce.

8. El nombre original de Antigua Guatemala era . . .

   a. La Real y Pontificia Ciudad de Guatemala.

   b. Santa Marta.

   c. Santiago de Guatemala.

   d. La Ciudad de Agua y Fuego.

9. La capital se trasladó al valle de la Ermita en . . .

a. 1763.	**c.** 1783.
b. 1773.	**d.** 1793.

10. Algo característico de las calles centrales de la Ciudad de Guatemala es que . . .

a. son empedradas.	**c.** hay muchas ruinas.
b. hay muchas iglesias.	**d.** hay muchos vendedores.

2-3. **Las ciudades.** As you watch the video, indicate with an **X** the city that matches the information in the left hand column. In some cases both cities may share the same characteristics.

	Antigua Guatemala	Ciudad Capital
Aquí la Semana Santa es muy importante.		
Tiene arquitectura colonial.		
Tiene calles empedradas.		
Tiene edificios grandes y modernos.		
Tiene muchas iglesias.		
Hay puestos comerciales en las calles.		
Tiene un elegante teatro con monumentos indígenas.		
Tiene tráfico ruidoso.		
Aquí se construyó una de las primeras universidades de América Latina.		
Tiene dos volcanes como parte de su paisaje.		

2-4. **Description.** Watch the segment on Antigua Guatemala or Guatemala City and describe an area, place or building that you find interesting. Write four to five complete sentences about what you see.

III. After Viewing

3-1. Comparisons. Work with a partner to compare and contrast Guatemala and the United States. Write at least five differences and similarities and then present the information to the class.

3-2. Writing Activity. A friend of yours who will be traveling to Guatemala writes you an e-mail in which he/she asks you to tell him about the country. Reply by writing about what you have learned after watching the video. Write five to six complete sentences.

3-3. Role play. With a classmate create a role play based on the situation outlined below. Use vocabulary that you have learned in the video.

STUDENT A: You are writing a paper on Guatemala, and your friend tells you that he/she just had a lesson about Guatemala in his/her Spanish class. Take a few minutes to prepare questions to ask your classmate.

STUDENT B: When talking to student A you find out that he/she is writing a paper on Guatemala, and you tell him/her that you just learned about this country in your Spanish class; so he/she proceeds to ask you questions. Provide as much information as possible.

IV. Class Activities

4-1. Temas.

Paso 1: In small groups, choose three of the following themes and draw a sketch that represents each of them.

- La variedad geográfica
- Indígenas y ladinos
- La herencia indígena maya
- La resistencia cultural indígena
- La contribución de los españoles
- Rigoberta Menchú
- La época colonial
- La religión católica
- Lo antiguo y lo moderno
- La importancia del cultivo del maíz
- [Any other theme you learned about in the video]

Paso 2: Write three complete sentences explaining or describing each theme. Use the information and vocabulary that you have learned in the video.

Paso 3: After completing **Pasos 1** and **2,** each group should do a two- to three-minute presentation for the entire class, describing the sketches and explaining why these themes are important to Guatemala.

Los hispanos en los Estados Unidos

INTRODUCTION

The video on Hispanics in the United States presents some basic information about this population and its growing influence on American culture. It also serves as an introduction to a small part of the rich and diverse cultural heritage of different Latino groups in this country. Some of the topics covered include traditional cuisine, music, dance, art, and sports.

USEFUL VOCABULARY

Nouns

minoría	*minority*	mayoría	*majority*
censo	*census*	avión	*plane*
país	*country*	terremoto	*earthquake*
baile	*dance*	desafío	*challenge*
vida	*life*	boda	*wedding*
iglesia	*church*	olla	*pot*
herencia	*heritage*	barro	*clay*
sitio	*site*	toro	*bull*
Salón de la Fama	*Hall of Fame*	dulces	*candy*
héroe	*hero*	palo	*stick*
deporte	*sport*	piso	*floor*

Verbs

traer	*to bring*	morir	*to die*
entretener	*to entertain*	tratar	*to try*
mantener	*to maintain*	romper	*to break*
mostrar	*to show*	mover	*to move*
poder	*to be able to*	pegar	*to hit*
pintar	*to paint*	caer	*to fall*
aprender	*to learn*	colaborar	*to collaborate*
divertirse	*to have fun*	enfrentar	*to face, to confront*
ayudar	*to help*		

Adjectives and other expressions

según	*according to*	arqueológico	*archeological*
numerosos	*numerous*	cubierta	*covered*
conocido	*known*	engomado	*with glue*
creciente	*growing*	llena	*full*

I. Before Viewing

1-1. **Influencia de hispanos.** Discuss as a class or in small groups the Hispanic presence and influence in the United States in the areas of cuisine, music, language, sports, entertainment, and politics.

1-2. **Diversidad de hispanos.** Write a list that includes the largest Hispanic groups in the United States and in what areas of the country they are concentrated. Are the groups the same or are there differences between them? If so, what are those differences? What is the largest Hispanic group in your part of the country?

II. While Viewing

2-1. Los deportes. As you watch the video, indicate in the chart below four Hispanic nationalities. For each nationality, list a sport that is popular within that group and a famous athlete mentioned in the video.

Nacionalidad	Deporte	Deportistas

2-2. Roberto Clemente. Based on the video segment about Roberto Clemente, answer the following questions.

1. For what major league team did Roberto Clemente play?

2. How long did he play for that team?

3. What was his most significant athletic achievement?

4. How did he die?

5. Why is he considered a hero among Hispanics?

2-3. **Bailes hispanos.** Watch the video segment on traditional Hispanic dances and then, with the video paused, describe the different clothes and their colors.

2-4. **Los murales hispanos.** Based on the video segment on murals, arrange the following statements in the order they appear in the video.

_______ En este mural se pueden ver algunos héroes de la Guerra de Independencia y de la Revolución.

_______ Un grupo de estudiantes hispanos se divierte y aprende mientras ayuda a pintar un mural.

_______ Hay murales que se pueden ver en varias ciudades como Los Ángeles, San Francisco, El Paso y Miami.

_______ Los mayas pintaron con brillantes colores la historia de sus guerras y sus victorias.

2-5. **Las comidas hispanas.** View the video segment on cuisine again and indicate next to each dish the order in which it appears.

Comida mexicana	orden	Comida puertorriqueña	orden
tostadas		alcapurrias	
salsas picantes		tostones	
mole		piraguas	
tacos		arroz con gandules	
frijoles refritos		bacalaitos	
totopos			
quesadillas			

III. After Viewing

3-1. **La piñata.** Some people have criticized **piñata** parties because they believe this type of party promotes violence from a very early age. They say **piñatas** make violence not only fun, but rewarding as well. What do you think? Have you ever attended a **piñata** party? How did the children behave?

3-2. **Una invitación.** Working with a partner design and write an invitation for a **piñata** party. Include information on activities and food at your party.

IV. Class Activities

4-1. **Hispanos famosos.** As a class, make a list of other famous U.S. Hispanics in the areas of television, movies, sports, music, and politics. Discuss their contributions to this country.

4-2. **La inmigración.** As a class, divide into three groups. Each group should discuss one of the topics listed below and then present its conclusions to the class. Based on these topics, discuss possible solutions to the immigration situation in the United States, especially as it concerns Hispanics.

a. positive aspects of immigration

b. negative aspects of immigration

c. solutions to the current immigration situation

México

INTRODUCTION

This video presents basic information on the Spanish-speaking country of Mexico, our neighboring country to the south. You will learn about Mexico's geography, pre-Columbian cultures, art, music, Revolution, and day-to-day life.

In order to do some of the exercises below, you will need to view the video as directed: all at once, by individual segments, or without the volume.

USEFUL VOCABULARY

mestizo	*a person of both Spanish and Native American heritage*
olmecas	*Olmecs, first civilization in Mesoamerica*
toltecas	*Toltecs, early civilization in Mesoamerica*
mayas	*Mayans, the most advanced of Mesoamerican civilizations*
aztecas	*Aztecs, conquerors of the Mayans*
cero	*zero*
maíz	*corn*
astronomía	*astronomy*
Quetzalcóatl	*also known as Kukulcán, the plumed serpent; god of knowledge, arts, and the morning star*
sabiduría	*wisdom and/or knowledge*
matinal	*morning*
desarrollar	*to develop*
sobresalir	*to surpass, to dominate*
lago	*lake*
elevado	*elevated*
cancha	*field, court*
a pesar de	*in spite of*
duodécima	*twelfth*
sin embargo	*nevertheless*
construir	*to construct*

conocimiento	*knowledge*	estrella	*star*
Teotihuacán	*capital of the Toltec empire*	imperio	*empire*
taparrabos	*loin cloth*	emigración	*emigration*
escalón	*step*	calabaza	*squash*
dios	*god*	frijoles	*beans*
herencia	*heritage*	algodón	*cotton*
calendario	*calendar*	ruinas	*ruins*
casi	*almost*	conquistar	*to conquest*
emplumada	*plumed, with feathers*	mural	*mural*

I. Before Viewing

1-1. Los hechos. What basic information do you already know about Mexico?

Paso 1. Write down what you know about Mexico, its culture, and its people: Do you know any famous Mexican writers, actors, or musicians? How many cities can you name? Who is the president of the nation? Can you name a famous artist?

	México
Escritor/a	
Músico	
Cantante	
Artista	
Político	
Celebración	
Ciudad	
Comida o producto típico	

Paso 2. With a group of classmates compare the information you have gathered about Mexico with information about your country. Then write a short paragraph in which you compare aspects of the two countries, such as famous people, geography, and languages. Comment among your classmates on similarities and differences between Mexico and your country.

II. While Viewing

2-1. Cierto o falso. Read the sentences and decide if they are true **(Cierto)** or false **(Falso)**.

	Cierto	Falso
1. México es un país que está lejos de los EE. UU.	❏	❏
2. Guatemala está al sur de México.	❏	❏
3. México tiene más de 100 millones de habitantes.	❏	❏
4. El Océano Pacífico está al oeste de México.	❏	❏
5. México es esencialmente elevado y montañoso.	❏	❏
6. Quetzalcóatl es el dios de la sabiduría.	❏	❏
7. Uxmal es una ciudad tolteca.	❏	❏
8. Los mayas eran grandes matemáticos.	❏	❏
9. Un ejemplo de la arquitectura colonial en México es la Universidad de México.	❏	❏
10. México tiene la quinta economía del mundo.	❏	❏

2-2. ¡A completar! Complete the following sentences with the words from the list below based on the information in the video.

México	Cortés	El maíz
Las cabezas grandes	El Palacio Nacional	Teotihuacán
El Templo del Adivino	Diego Rivera	
Los mayas	Tenochtitlán	

1. ___________________ representan a los reyes de la cultura olmeca.

2. ___________________ es tres veces más grande que el estado de Texas.

3. ___________________ era la ciudad religiosa de los toltecas conocida como la ciudad donde los hombres se convertían en dioses.

4. ___________________ era la comida básica de los olmecas.

5. ___________________ está en Uxmal.

6. ___________________ desarrollaron el concepto del cero.

7. ___________________ era la capital azteca donde hoy está construida la ciudad de México.

8. _____________________ conquistó el imperio azteca.

9. _____________________ fue construido sobre las casas antiguas de Moctezuma.

10. _____________________ pintó en sus murales la historia de México.

III. After Viewing

3-1. Ensalada de palabras.

Paso 1. Working with a partner, organize the following words into three groups. Assign a category or title to each group and then present them to the class.

olmecas	mayas	independencia	la Conquista
Palacio	murales	astronomía	maíz
Nacional	idioma español	Diego Rivera	Cortés
toltecas	Teotihuacán	Universidad de	aztecas
pirámides	Revolución	México	
catedral	mexicana	periodo de la	
templos	Zapata	Colonia	

Grupo 1:	Grupo 2:	Grupo 3:

3-2. Visita a México. With a classmate, create a schedule for one week in Teotihuacán, Uxmal, and Mexico City. Consult the Internet for general information on Mexico. Next, choose your itinerary including places, activities, and times of day.

	Lugar	Actividad
lunes		
martes		
miércoles		
jueves		
viernes		
sábado		
domingo		

3-3. Los mayas. Research the Mayan numeral system and present your findings to the class. Create questions for the class on this topic. For example, you could request that your classmates read Mayan numerals as you write them on the board.

3-4. Una entrevista. With a classmate, imagine you are interviewing a person from Mexico who knows a lot about that country. Ask him or her about the pre-Columbian cultures that you see on the video. First, create a list of questions and then write a dialogue to present to the class.

4-1. **Feria cultural.** In groups of three or four write a brochure for an aspect of Mexican culture that interests you. It might be a pre-Columbian ruin, a religious festival, or an event in Mexican history. Each group in the class will present its work and either answer questions of the class or move about from group to group asking questions.

Paso 1. First, watch the video again for comprehension and to choose an aspect of Mexican culture for your brochure. Then, prepare an outline on the issues you want to investigate. Finally, consult the Internet to research some of the information you need. Find out:

1. Basic information about Mexico

2. The topic you want to present

3. Relevant facts about it

4. Why it is interesting/fun/important/relevant

5. How people can learn more about it

Paso 2. Create the brochure with your group. You may use construction paper and magazine pictures to enhance your brochure.

4-2. **Un personaje famoso en EE.UU.** Research a famous Mexican whose life was, or still is, connected to the United States, either by his or her impact on American culture or history or American culture's influence on that person. For example, Octavio Paz, author of *The Labyrinth of Solitude*. Present the most important aspects of your research to your classmates.

Nicaragua, El Salvador y Honduras

INTRODUCTION

This video presents information about Nicaragua, El Salvador and Honduras, all of which are Spanish-speaking countries in Central America. You will learn about these countries' geography, history, people, and culture, as well as their cuisine and tourism.

USEFUL VOCABULARY

desempleo	*unemployment*	maduro	*ripe*
a pesar de	*despite*	tiburones	*sharks*
mientras que	*while*	buceo	*scuba diving*
antes	*before*	peces	*fish*
contaminación	*pollution*	fértiles	*fertile*
izquierdista	*left wing*	hermosos	*beautiful*
rellena	*filled*	creciendo	*growing*
revueltos	*mixed*	meta	*goal*

I. Before Viewing

1-1. Geografía. Look at the map of Central America at the beginning of the video. Identify Nicaragua, El Salvador and Honduras. What are some of the features of these countries? What do you know about these countries?

II. While Viewing

2-1. Clima. Describe the weather in each of the regions featured in the video.

2-2. Comida nacional. Plan a Central American dinner based on the typical foods from Nicaragua, El Salvador and Honduras that you saw in the video.

2-3. Turismo. Plan a one-week vacation to Central America. What places would you visit? How long would you stay in each place?

2-4. ¿Similares o diferentes? Compare the following characteristics of each country as described in the video.

	Nicaragua	El Salvador	Honduras
Geografía			
Comida			
Turismo			

III. After Viewing

3-1. Mi opinión. Write a short paragraph in which you give your general opinion of one of these three Central American countries. Would you like to live there for a semester? Why or why not?

3-2. Comparaciones. Compare one of these countries with your own country. What differences and similarities are there between the two?

IV. Class Activities

You and your classmates have just returned from a trip to Nicaragua, El Salvador and Honduras. In groups of three to five, prepare a report on your experience. What was it like? What did you learn? What did you eat?

Consult the Internet to research one of the writers mentioned in the video. Choose one of his or her poems and present it to the class.

Panamá

INTRODUCTION

This video presents basic information about Panamá, one of the countries in Central America where Spanish is spoken. You will learn information about Panamá's geography, economy, art, traditions, and every day life. We hope you enjoy this presentation.

In order to do some of the exercises below, you will need to view the video as directed: all at once, by individual segments, or without the volume.

USEFUL VOCABULARY

Expresiones

¡Ven a visitarnos!	*Come visit us!*
¡No lo vas a olvidar!	*You won't forget it*

Productos

plátano	*banana*
pesca	*fishery*
caña de azúcar	*sugar cane*
madera	*timber, wood*
café	*coffee*
chibcha	*language of the indigenous people called Kunas*

Idiomas

español	*Spanish*

Otras palabras

mestizo	*a person of mixed Spanish and indigenous heritage*
iglesia	*church*
altar	*altar*
portada	*frontispiece, entrance, front cover*
prócer	*founding father*
ecoturismo	*ecotourism*

I. Before Viewing

1-1. Los hechos. What do you know about Panamá? Record what you know about its culture and its people: Do you know any famous Panamanian politicians, founding fathers (**próceres**) or musicians? How many cities can you name? Who is the president of the nation? Can you name a famous artist? Can you name an important and famous canal in Panamá?

Prócer	
Músico/a	
Presidente	
Ciudad	
Producto típico	
Canal importante	

1-2. Ensalada de palabras.

Paso 1. With a partner, group the following words into three categories. Assign a theme or title to each group.

costa	océano	bohío
bosque	biodiversidad	chibcha
canal	cascada	piraguas
mar	esclusa	istmo
trópico	playa	locomotora
nave	kunas	molas

Grupo 1	Grupo 2	Grupo 3

Paso 2. Make sure you know the meanings of these words. You may use your dictionary if necessary. Working in groups, decide which of these words are related to your culture or to a culture in your country. For example, is there a minority that speaks Chibcha in the United States? Is there a colonial church nearby or in your town? Present information on five of these concepts to the class.

II. While Viewing

2-1. ¿Qué sabes sobre Panamá? Watch the first five minutes of the video again. Determine if the following statements are true (**Cierto**) or false (**Falso**) based on your knowledge about Panamá, its culture and history, and what you have seen and heard in the video.

1. Panamá es un país de Centroamérica.

   ❏ **Cierto**   ❏ **Falso**

2. Panamá limita al oeste con los Estados Unidos.

   ❏ **Cierto**   ❏ **Falso**

3. Panamá es un país grande y tiene más de 100 millones de habitantes.

   ❏ **Cierto**   ❏ **Falso**

4. La mayoría de los panameños son indígenas y blancos.

   ❏ **Cierto**   ❏ **Falso**

5. El Canal de Panamá pertenece a los Estados Unidos desde 1999.

   ❏ **Cierto**   ❏ **Falso**

6. El Mar Caribe está al norte de Panamá.

   ❏ **Cierto**   ❏ **Falso**

7. En Panamá el clima es frío y poco soleado.

   ❏ **Cierto**   ❏ **Falso**

8. El Canal de Panamá une el Océano Pacífico con el Mar Caribe.

   ❏ **Cierto**   ❏ **Falso**

9. La Zona Libre de Colón es un centro comercial de importancia mundial.

   ❏ **Cierto**   ❏ **Falso**

10. En Panamá se habla español, chibcha e inglés.

   ❏ **Cierto**   ❏ **Falso**

2-2. Temas.

Paso 1. Watch the entire video and with a classmate make a list of the topics you can recall. Can you come up with at least five topics?

Paso 2. Now, compare topics with another group of students. Choose a specific topic and consult the Internet to find out more about it. For example, you may try to find information about the Panama Canal, Colonial architecture in Panamá or the names of some Panamanian musicians. Prepare a brief report on your findings to present to the class.

Paso 3. The Panamanian national dress is the **pollera**. Looking at the images again, write an e-mail to a friend telling her/him how **polleras** are made, and then design your own **pollera** with the embroidery designs you like best. You may try to design a **pollera estadounidense** using designs typical of your culture. What would you put on it? What colors would you use? (You may choose to do this activity on the **mola**, a typical Panamanian handicraft.)

III. After Viewing

3-1. Horario de vacaciones.

Paso 1. With a classmate, create a schedule for a one-day visit to a Panamanian City. First, discuss with your classmate differences in languages and other cultural aspects. Consult the Internet to find information on what Panamanians eat, their store hours, and sightseeing itineraries.

Now choose the city or town in which you will stay and the activities you will do there. Make sure you record times of day, types of transportation, meals, leisure activities, at least one cultural site, and an evening activity.

Paso 2. Discuss your schedule with two other pairs of students. Decide what type of tourists you are, based on the selection of your activities. Are you adventurous (**aventurero/a**)? Classy (**sofisticado/a**)? Describe the other groups' styles as well. Use verbs like **gustar, molestar, importar, querer,** and **desear**.

3-2. **Una entrevista.** With a classmate, imagine you are interviewing a Panamanian whose job is related to something you saw in the video. For example, you could interview a vendor at a street market, a woman who is embroidering a **mola**, a worker at the Panama Canal, a salsa musician, or an entrepreneur.

Paso 1. First make a list of questions you would like to ask the person in relation to his or her job or activity.

Paso 2. Now create a role-play in which one person is the interviewer and the other is the interviewee. Present your dialogue to the class. Make sure your dialogue includes some of the information you have seen or heard in the video.

3-3. **Un viaje inolvidable.**

Paso 1. View the video segment subtitled **Los kunas**. Then, answer the following questions in groups.

1. ¿Desde cuándo llevan viviendo en Panamá los indígenas kunas?

2. ¿Qué idioma hablan los indios kunas aparte del español?

3. ¿En qué se parece el gobierno de la Comarca Kuna-Yala a la soberanía tribal de los indios en los Estados Unidos?

4. ¿Cuáles son las similitudes y diferencias entre los indios kunas y los indios de los Estados Unidos?

5. ¿Por qué la Comarca Kuna-Yala ofrece la oportunidad de viajar al pasado?

6. Observa las artesanías. ¿Has visto en tu comunidad objetos parecidos? ¿Cuáles?

4-1. **Un personaje famoso en EE.UU.** Research a famous Panamanian whose life was, or still connected to the United States. For instance, Panamanian President Omar Torrijos signed treaties with American President Jimmy Carter, and many American and Panamanian scientists work together at the Smithsonian Tropical Research Institute in Panama City. Present the most important aspects of your research to your classmates.

El Perú

INTRODUCTION

This video presents basic information about Peru, a country in South America with many interesting places to visit. Get ready to enjoy the trip!

USEFUL VOCABULARY

adoración	*worship*	selva	*rainforest*
autopista	*highway*	terraza	*terrace*
barrio	*neighborhood*	terremoto	*earthquake*
conquista	*conquest*	tesoro	*treasure*
diversidad	*diversity*	tierra	*land*
dominar	*dominate*	andino	*Andean*
fuego	*fire*	antiguo	*ancient*
rasgo	*trait*	arqueológico	*archeological*
riqueza	*wealth*	precolombino	*precolombian*
retiro	*withdrawal*	espárrago	*asparagus*
ruina	*ruin*		

I. Before Viewing

1-1. **What do you know about Peru?** Write what you know about its culture and its people, for example, its capital, currency, location, industries, or languages. As you watch the beginning segment of the video see how many things you can identify.

II. While Viewing

2-1. **Vocabulario.** As you watch the video on Peru write down words or phrases you can understand. Group them according to their linguistic functions.

Adjetivos	Sustantivos	Verbos

2-2. Machu Picchu. Indicate whether the following sentences about Machu Picchu are true (**Cierto**) or false (**Falso**) based on the information in the video. Correct statements that are false.

1. También se llama Ciudad Perdida.

   ❏ **Cierto**   ❏ **Falso**

   ____

2. Son ruinas de la época pre-incaica.

   ❏ **Cierto**   ❏ **Falso**

   ____

3. "Inti" es una palabra de origen aymara.

   ❏ **Cierto**   ❏ **Falso**

   ____

4. Machu Pichu se ubica en la cordillera de los Andes.

   ❏ **Cierto**   ❏ **Falso**

   ____

5. Los españoles destruyeron Machu Picchu.

   ❏ **Cierto**   ❏ **Falso**

   ____

6. La arquitectura de Machu Picchu sorprende a muchas personas.

   ❏ **Cierto**   ❏ **Falso**

   ____

2-3. La conquista de los incas. Use the words in the box to complete the summary of the Spaniards' arrival to Peru.

primero   pero   finalmente

además   por lo tanto

El contacto de los europeos con los nativos ocurrió (1)_______________ en el Caribe. Los españoles buscaban oro, metales y querían expandir su territorio de dominio. (2)_______________ usaron la religión católica como excusa para invadir América. La conquista causó un choque cultural muy grande (3)_______________ los resultados fueron trágicos. (4)_______________, con la llegada de los españoles llegaron nuevas enfermedades. Muchos nativos murieron. (5)_______________, Pizarro fundó la ciudad de Lima como la nueva capital del imperio.

2-4. Regiones geográficas. Write down the geographical region of Peru associated with each description.

1. Es un lugar de producción de plantas.   _______________________

2. Hay muchas playas hermosas.   _______________________

3. Las montañas son altas y hay muchos animales. _______________________

III. After Viewing

3-1. Diversidad étnica. Working in groups, discuss the reasons for Peru's great racial, linguistic, and cultural diversity.

3-2. Lima. Describe Lima, Peru's capital. In which parts of the city are the more modern areas located?

3-3. Comparaciones. Based on the narration, compare the history of the Native Americans from the United States to those from Peru. Are their histories similar or different? Why?

4-1. Un viaje a Perú. You and your classmates are going to Peru! Make a list of 10 to 12 questions that you could ask people to get more information about this country. If you and/or your classmates actually know people from Peru, they would be the perfect subjects for this project.

Puerto Rico

INTRODUCTION

This video is about Puerto Rico, one of the Caribbean islands where Spanish is spoken. Puerto Rico is a commonwealth of the United States and Puerto Ricans are U.S. citizens. In this video, you will learn about Puerto Rico's geography, traditions, cuisine, and everyday life. The island is known to all as **La Isla del Encanto**—The Island of Enchantment.

USEFUL VOCABULARY

Nouns

el arroz	*rice*
el baloncesto	*basketball*
el béisbol	*baseball*
los bomberos	*firefighters*
el borinquen, la borinqueña	*Puerto Rican*
el boxeo	*boxing*
el dominó	*dominos*
el español	*Spanish*
la fortaleza	*fort*
las habichuelas	*beans*
el inglés	*English*
la isla	*island*
el jefe	*chief*
el Mar Caribe	*Caribbean Sea*
los mariscos	*shellfish*
las montañas	*mountains*
el Parque de Bombas	*name of fire station in Ponce, Puerto Rico*
los plátanos	*plantains*
la playa	*beach*
el pollo	*chicken*

el/la puertorriqueño/a	*Puerto Rican*
el río	*river*
los taínos	*the indigenous people of Puerto Rico*
el Viejo San Juan	*Old San Juan*

Adjectives

antiguo/a	*old, antique*
clásico/a	*classical*
elegante	*elegant*
famoso/a	*famous*
misterioso/a	*mysterious*
nuevo/a	*new*
oscuro/a	*dark*
otro/a	*another*
tropical	*tropical*
viejo/a	*old*

I. Before Viewing

1-1. Los hechos. Based on what you know about Puerto Rico, answer the following questions:

1. What languages are spoken in Puerto Rico?

2. What is the capital of Puerto Rico?

3. Indicate with a check mark the Puerto Rican foods you have tasted.

    _____Rice and beans

    _____Tostones (fried plantains)

    _____Perníl (pork roast)

    _____Flan (custard dessert)

    _____Other ____

4. Baseball is a very popular sport in Puerto Rico. Do you know any famous Puerto Rican baseball players? If so, who?

II. While Viewing

2-1. La Isla. Skim the following statements to get an idea of the content. Then, as you are viewing the video, circle the letter that correctly completes each one.

1. Puerto Rico es . . .

   a. una isla.

   b. un país en la Península Ibérica.

   c. una ciudad en Europa.

2. Puerto Rico está . . .

   a. entre el Mar Caribe y el Océano Pacífico.

   b. entre el Mar Caribe y el Océano Atlántico.

   c. en los Estados Unidos.

3. En Puerto Rico . . .

   a. se habla solamente inglés.

   b. se habla solamente español.

   c. se habla inglés y español.

4. *El Morro* es . . .

   a. una fortaleza.

   b. una casa.

   c. una religión.

5. El *Parque de Bombas* es . . .

   a. un estadio de juegos.

   b. una playa grande.

   c. una estación de bomberos.

6. El *Observatorio de Arecibo* . . .

   a. tiene el radiotelescopio más pequeño del mundo.

   b. tiene el radiotelescopio más grande del mundo.

   c. busca inteligencia extraterrestre en los Estados Unidos.

7. Los taínos son . . .

   a. una tribu indígena.

   b. los puertorriqueños jóvenes de hoy día.

   c. los españoles que vinieron a la isla con Cristóbal Colón.

8. El mofongo se hace con . . .

   a. manzanas.

   b. plátanos verdes.

   c. pollo.

9. A los puertorriqueños . . .

   a. les gusta jugar al béisbol y al baloncesto.

   b. les gustan los juegos acuáticos.

   c. a y b

10. Puerto Rico es el centro universal de la música . . .

   a. salsa.

   b. tango.

   c. jazz.

2-2. **Más información.** Now expand on this information by adding one more fact to each of the statements in exercise 2-1. View the video again if necessary.

III. After Viewing

3-1. Comparaciones. Indicate if the following statements are true (**Cierto**) or false (**Falso**), based on the information in the video. Correct any false statements.

1. Puerto Rico es una isla entre el Mar Caribe y el Océano Atlántico.

   ❒ **Cierto**   ❒ **Falso**

   ____

2. En Puerto Rico se habla solamente español.

   ❒ **Cierto**   ❒ **Falso**

   ____

3. Cristóbal Colón descubrió Puerto Rico.

   ❒ **Cierto**   ❒ **Falso**

   ____

4. *Ponce* es la capital de Puerto Rico.

   ❒ **Cierto**   ❒ **Falso**

   ____

5. La fortaleza *El Morro* fue construida para defender San Juan de los piratas.

   ❒ **Cierto**   ❒ **Falso**

   ____

6. El *Parque de Bombas* no fue una estación de bomberos.

   ❒ **Cierto**   ❒ **Falso**

   ____

7. A los puertorriqueños les gusta comer arroz con habichuelas.

   ❒ **Cierto**   ❒ **Falso**

   ____

8. El flan es un postre muy popular en Puerto Rico.

   ❒ **Cierto**   ❒ **Falso**

   ____

9. A los puertorriqueños no les gusta el béisbol.

☐ **Cierto**   ☐ **Falso**

___

10. La música *salsa* nació en España.

☐ **Cierto**   ☐ **Falso**

___

3-2. **Temas.** Choose one of the following topics and write a brief paragraph on it.

1. Would you like to visit Puerto Rico? If so, what would you like to see?

2. What Puerto Rican foods would you like to taste and why?

3. Do you like *salsa* music? Do you know how to dance *salsa?* If not, would you like to learn?

IV. Class Activities

4-1. **Un viaje a Puerto Rico.** You and a friend are planning a trip to Puerto Rico and would like to make a list of the places and activities that interest you. Think about what you have seen in the video and consult the Internet to plan a stay of three nights and four days on the island. You may include sporting and cultural events, cuisine, and outdoor activities, to name a few.

4-2. Crucigrama. Complete the following puzzle with the Spanish equivalent of the given words. Do not repeat words. Use the **Useful Vocabulary** section as a reference.

Down	Across	Crossword Puzzle
1. Puerto Rican	1. chicken	
2. Caribbean	2. tropical	
3. to drink	3. sport	
4. to eat	4. pork	
5. to eat dinner	5. elegant	
6. type of dance	6. baseball	
7. was born	7. to laugh	
8. English	8. island	
9. indigenous group	9. chief	
10. sun	10. river	
11. rice	11. another	
14. fire	12. firemen	
15. old	13. plantains	
16. antique	14. new	
17. classic	15. only	
18. famous	16. fort	
	17. dark	
	18. more	
	19. to play	
	20. coffee	
	21. tasty	
	22. heat	

La República Dominicana

INTRODUCTION

The video you are about to view presents basic information on the Dominican Republic, one of the Caribbean countries where Spanish is spoken. You will learn about the Dominican Republic's geography, economy, traditions, cuisine, and everyday life. We hope you enjoy this presentation.

USEFUL VOCABULARY

merengue	*the national popular dance of the Dominican Republic*
carnaval	*carnival*
patrona del país	*patron saint*
diablos cojuelos	*characters from the Dominican carnival;* diablos cojuelos *costumes are very colorful and include a scary mask*
taínos	*indigenous tribe from the West Indies*
amistosa	*friendly*
hospitalaria	*hospitable*
rapel	*rappel*
parapente	*paragliding*
puro	*cigar*
arroz	*rice*
habichuelas	*beans*
guisada	*stew*
plátano	*plantain*
frito	*fried*
sancocho	*soup made of different types of meats and vegetables*
parrilla	*grill*
salsa criolla	*creole sauce*

1-1. Vocabulary Review.

Paso 1. Word Search. Find the following words.

CARNAVAL	REGALO	PLAYA	SONRISA	CRISTALINA
SOL	RITMO	TERRITORIO	LANGOSTA	MONUMENTO
ARTESANÍA	TIBIO	MERENGUE	PURO	COLORIDO

```
C  A  R  N  A  V  A  L  P  S  A  S  C  U  C
O  G  W  Y  P  U  R  O  X  E  I  M  A  S  O
O  L  A  G  E  R  M  S  O  C  N  P  T  I  L
V  L  C  A  M  C  K  T  F  X  A  I  S  H  O
P  U  M  Q  O  E  N  C  O  X  S  V  O  S  R
S  P  O  T  A  E  T  H  I  H  E  V  G  Q  I
W  M  H  M  M  N  Z  T  B  J  T  G  N  T  D
M  W  Q  U  T  S  I  S  I  K  R  Z  A  R  O
S  E  N  T  R  I  O  L  T  C  A  F  L  G  L
E  O  R  H  I  N  R  W  A  I  X  Q  Q  F  Z
M  M  L  E  R  O  I  R  O  T  I  R  R  E  T
M  W  Q  I  N  B  G  E  E  L  S  L  X  G  K
F  Y  S  N  U  G  O  K  M  Z  Y  I  P  M  T
R  A  P  C  D  C  U  S  R  V  V  O  R  H  P
Z  Z  Q  D  C  T  K  E  A  Z  S  Z  A  C  X
```

Paso 2. Look up the meanings of the words above in a dictionary. Then, with a group of students, write a short story of at least eight to ten complete sentences using as many of the words from the list as you can. Read your story aloud to the class. As your classmates listen they should write down the words from the list they can identify.

1-2. Los hechos.

Paso 1. La República Dominicana. What do you know about the Dominican Republic? Complete the following chart with the information you know.

La República Dominicana	
IDIOMA	
RELIGIÓN MAYORITARIA	
RAZAS Y GRUPOS ÉTNICOS	
CIUDAD CAPITAL	
DEPORTES FAVORITOS	
MÚSICA TRADICIONAL	
PERSONAJES FAMOSOS	

II. While Viewing

2-1. ¿Qué sabes sobre la República Dominicana? Determine if the following statements are true (**Cierto**) or false (**Falso**) based on what you have seen and heard in the video. Correct any false statements.

1. La República Dominicana está situada en América del Sur.

❏ **Cierto**　　❏ **Falso**

____

2. La capital de la República Dominicana es San José.

❏ **Cierto**　　❏ **Falso**

____

3. Los españoles descubrieron la isla de Quisqueya en 1492.

❏ **Cierto**　　❏ **Falso**

____

4. En la República Dominicana se producen aceitunas, manzanas, y vino.

❏ **Cierto**　　❏ **Falso**

____

5. El plato tradicional de la cocina dominicana tiene arroz, habichuelas, carne, y plátanos fritos.

    ❏ Cierto   ❏ Falso

____

6. Los diablos cojuelos son personajes del carnaval de La Vega.

    ❏ Cierto   ❏ Falso

____

7. En la República Dominicana hay muchos edificios de la época colonial.

    ❏ Cierto   ❏ Falso

____

8. Muchos peloteros dominicanos juegan en equipos americanos de las grandes ligas.

    ❏ Cierto   ❏ Falso

____

9. Actualmente la República Dominicana disfruta de un régimen democrático.

    ❏ Cierto   ❏ Falso

____

2-2. Temas.

Paso 1. Working with a classmate, watch the video again in its entirety. Then, make a list of the topics you recall. Try to remember at least five. Finally, write one or two particular details you remember about each.

Paso 2. Now, compare your list of topics with another group's. Choose a specific topic and consult the Internet to find out more about it. For instance, you may try to find information about Dominican tourist resorts, well-known Dominican people, the **Taíno** culture, Dominican music, or sports that are popular on the island. Next write a brief report on your findings to present to the class.

2-3. La playas dominicanas. Based on the images from the video, write an e-mail to a friend describing to him or her how beautiful the beaches in the Dominican Republic are. Be sure to use some of the new vocabulary you learned in this chapter.

III. After Viewing

3-1. Una entrevista. You and a classmate have been chosen by the local TV program *Música latina internacional* to interview Juan Luis Guerra, the famous Dominican composer and singer. Work with a classmate to prepare for the interview.

Paso 1. Consult the Internet to find information about Juan Luis Guerra and his group **4-40**. Make sure to listen to some of his most popular hits, as you might want to prepare some of the interview questions based on his songs.

Paso 2. Prepare eight to ten questions you would ask Juan Luis Guerra to find out about his background, his personality, and his music.

IV. Class Activities

4-1. Los dominicanos en EE.UU.

Paso 1. Consult the Internet to find information about the one million Dominicans living in the eastern part of the United States.

- Where are the Dominican communities located?
- What are some interesting and important facts about this group?
- Research some famous Dominicans in the United States, like Julia Alvarez, a talented Dominican-American author, and Oscar de la Renta, a famous Dominican fashion designer.
- What are some comparisons between the Dominican and American cultures?

Paso 2. Un artículo. Based on your research, prepare an outline focusing on the topics that interest you the most. Then, use your outline to write an article on the Dominican Republic. You may use photos or artwork to enhance your article.

4-3. Los bailes latinos. Is there a Latin dance group at your school? If so, have you ever been to one of their meetings or events? You can learn Latin dancing by starting with **merengue**, the most popular dance and music style in the Dominican Republic. Consult the Internet to find information on this popular style of dance and music—or another traditional Latin American dance like **cumbia**, **tango**, **salsa**, or **vallenato**—and write a brief description of it to present to the class. Include an audio component with your presentation and play some music for your classmates.

Uruguay

INTRODUCTION

The video you are going to see is about Uruguay, a Latin American country where Spanish is spoken. You will learn about Uruguay's geography, population, economy, culture, and daily life. In order for you to get the most enjoyment out of this video, we recommend that you view it all at once, by specific segments, or with the volume turned off, according to the directions in the activities.

USEFUL VOCABULARY

Expresiones

cebar mate	*to pour water into the mate gourd*
llegar al fin	*to finish something*
Mercado Común del Sur	*Southern Common Market*
mesa de los domingos	*Sunday family meal*
puerta de salida	*exit door*
¡Qué bien huele!	*That smells good!*

Productos y comidas

asado	*broiled beef ribs cut in a strip lengthwise*
cuero	*leather*
mariscos	*seafood*
lana	*wool*
mate	*a tea-like beverage, also the name of the hollow gourd used as a container for brewing the mate tea*
oveja	*sheep*
vaca	*cow*

Fiestas, tradiciones, y música

carnaval	*carnival*
llamadas	*calls*
murga	*carnival musical ensemble*
tambor	*drum*
rambla	*boulevard close to the shore, appropriate for leisure walking*
vida nocturna	*nightlife*
peatonal	*pedestrian*

I. Before Viewing

1-1. Los hechos. Complete the table below to indicate what you know about different aspects of Uruguay.

	Uruguay
ESCRITOR/A	
ARTISTA	
POLÍTICO/A	
COMIDA O PRODUCTO TÍPICO	
CIUDAD Y/O BALNEARIO	
FIESTAS Y CELEBRACIONES	

II. While Viewing

2-1. **¿Qué sabes sobre Uruguay?** Watch the first five minutes of the video once again. Determine if the following statements are true (**Cierto**) or false (**Falso**) based on your knowledge about Uruguay, its culture and history, and what you have seen and heard in the video. Correct any false statements.

1. En Uruguay hay un clima tropical.

   ❏ **Cierto**   ❏ **Falso**

   ____

2. La capital del Uruguay es Buenos Aires.

   ❏ **Cierto**   ❏ **Falso**

   ____

3. La ganadería es muy importante en la economía del Uruguay.

   ❏ **Cierto**   ❏ **Falso**

   ____

4. Uruguay no forma parte del Mercosur.

   ❏ **Cierto**   ❏ **Falso**

   ____

5. La Argentina está al Sur del Uruguay.

   ❏ **Cierto**   ❏ **Falso**

   ____

2-2. **Temas.**

Paso 1. Working with a classmate, watch the video again in its entirety. Then make a list of the topics you can recall. Can you come up with at least five topics and one or two particular details you remember about each one?

Paso 2. Now compare your list of topics with another group's. Choose a specific topic and consult the Internet to find out more about it. For instance, you may try to find a recipe for **chimichurri**, pictures of **murgas** or information about Uruguayan artists. Next write a brief report on your findings to present to the class.

2-3. Ensalada de palabras.

Paso 1. Working with a partner, organize the following words from the video into these three categories: **(1) Música, celebraciones y deportes; (2) Comidas y bebidas;** and **(3) Lugares y productos.**

candombe	asado	playa	ciclismo	tambores
balneario	rambla	llamadas	mate	ovejas
tango	murga	vacas	carnaval	fútbol

Paso 2. Make sure you know the meanings of these words; you can use a dictionary if necessary. Now decide which of these words are related to your culture or to a culture in your country. For example, in your country is there a traditional parade rooted in African culture? Is there a very popular beverage? Are soccer and biking very popular sports? Present your comparisons to the class.

2-4. Comidas y bebidas. Watch the video segment related to food and mate.

Paso 1. Complete the following paragraph with information you hear and see in the video.

Las comidas típicas uruguayas son de carne de (1)______________. Uno de los platos más populares es la parrillada. Otros platos típicos son el (2) ______________, y el (3) ______________. En el famoso (4) ______________ podemos probar estas delicias. ¡Qué bien huele! Sin embargo, los vegetarianos prefieren las ricas (5) ______________. En la costa del país abundan platos con (6) ______________ y (7) ______________.

Paso 2. Look again at the images where people are drinking **mate**, then consult the Internet for information about this beverage. Then, write an e-mail to a friend describing what **mate** is and any other aspect—historical or social, for example—of the beverage that you find interesting.

III. After Viewing

3-1. Entrevista. Is there a Uruguayan or another Hispanic restaurant or business in your neighborhood or town? Do you know a Spanish-speaking person in your school or community? Find a Spanish-speaking person to interview and ask him or her questions that apply to your community or to his or her role and circumstances in the community. Present your results to the whole class: describe the person and comment on his or her answers to your questions.

3-2. Una noche inolvidable.

Paso 1. View the video segment related to **Fiestas y celebraciones**. In groups, answer the following questions and discuss your ideas and opinions on this topic.

1. ¿Qué momento del día es?

2. ¿Qué crees que están celebrando?

3. ¿Crees que es una celebración formal/informal/de vecinos/étnica?

4. ¿Cómo son las personas que tocan y las que bailan?

5. ¿Qué tipo de ropa llevan los hombres y mujeres que tocan el tambor (tamborileros)?

Paso 2. Choose a picture that presents a typical American celebration. Following the questions presented above (see **Paso 1**), write an editorial column describing cultural differences and similarities between this American celebration and one from Uruguay. Rely on what you know from your own experience and what you have seen and heard in the video. Present your column to the class or to a group of students.

4-1. Un personaje famoso en EE.UU. Research an important or well-known Uruguayan whose life was, or still is, connected to the United States, either by his or her impact on American culture or history, or American culture's influence on that person. For example, the singer and composer Jorge Drexler received the 2005 *Best Original Song Academy Award* for **Al otro lado del río,** a song that was included in the soundtrack of "The Motorcycle Diaries," a popular film in the United States. Once you have completed your research, present what you have learned to your classmates.

Venezuela

INTRODUCTION

This video presents information about Venezuela, a South American country of many contrasts where you can find beautiful beaches, high mountains, deserts, jungles, and plains. You will learn about interesting aspects of Venezuela's geography, history, food, people, and music.

I. Before Viewing

1-1. Vocabulario útil. Before watching the video, read the following words and put a check mark next to those you recognize.

NOMBRE OFICIAL		GENTE	
CAPITAL		ARTE	
REGIONES		HISTORIA	
POBLACIÓN		INDUSTRIA	
CLIMA		MASA	
IDIOMA		MÚSICA	

1-2. ¿Qué sabes de Venezuela? Before watching the video, circle the correct answers to the questions below in order to test your knowledge about Venezuela.

   1. ¿Cuál es la capital de Venezuela?

      a. Bogotá

      b. Caracas

      c. Lima

2. ¿Dónde está Venezuela?

    a. en Suramérica

    b. en Centroamérica

    c. en Norteamérica

3. ¿Qué idioma se habla en Venezuela?

    a. español y portugués

    b. español y otras lenguas indígenas

    c. español

4. ¿Cuál es la moneda de Venezuela?

    a. el dólar

    b. el peso

    c. el bolívar

5. ¿Cuál es el producto principal de exportación de Venezuela?

    a. la banana

    b. el petróleo

    c. el maíz

II. While Viewing

2-1. La geografía de Venezuela. Match the following Venezuelan landmarks with their English definitions.

1. _____ Los Andes	**a.** jungle
2. _____ La Isla de Margarita	**b.** plains
3. _____ El Lago de Maracaibo	**c.** island
4. _____ Los Médanos	**d.** lake
5. _____ Caracas	**e.** mountains
6. _____ Canaima	**f.** capital
7. _____ Los Llanos	**g.** waterfall
8. _____ El Salto Ángel	**h.** desert

2-2. A completar. Fill the blanks with the correct words from the list below based on the information from the video.

conquistador	boleto	masa	libertador
ciudad	arepas	capital	tráfico

1. Los venezolanos comen _________________ para el desayuno, el almuerzo y la cena.

2. La _________________ para las arepas se hace con harina de maíz, agua y sal.

3. Simón Bolívar es el _________________ de Venezuela, Colombia, Perú, Ecuador y Bolivia.

4. La _________________ de Venezuela es Caracas.

5. En Caracas hay mucho _________________ por eso la gente prefiere usar el metro.

III. After Viewing

3-1. Cierto o falso. Read the following statements and decide whether they are true (**Cierto**) or false (**Falso**). Correct any false statements.

1. Venezuela tiene aproximadamente 25 millones de habitantes.

   ❑ **Cierto**   ❑ **Falso**

   ____

2. Américo Vespucio llegó a Venezuela y vio las casas de los indígenas sobre el agua.

   ❑ **Cierto**   ❑ **Falso**

   ____

3. Venezuela quiere decir "pequeña Venecia".

   ❑ **Cierto**   ❑ **Falso**

   ____

4. Simón Bolívar era un conquistador español.

   ❑ **Cierto**   ❑ **Falso**

   ____

5. En Caracas no hay mucho tráfico.

❑ **Cierto**   ❑ **Falso**

____

6. Las arepas, las cachapas y la carne son sitios de Venezuela.

❑ **Cierto**   ❑ **Falso**

____

7. El cuatro es un instrumento musical típico de Venezuela.

❑ **Cierto**   ❑ **Falso**

____

8. En Los Andes nieva.

❑ **Cierto**   ❑ **Falso**

____

9. Los españoles nunca esclavizaron a los indígenas.

❑ **Cierto**   ❑ **Falso**

____

10. Simón Bolívar liberó a Venezuela, Colombia, Perú, Bolivia y Ecuador.

❑ **Cierto**   ❑ **Falso**

____

3-2. **Una carta.** Write a letter to a friend telling him or her that you plan to visit Venezuela in the summer. Mention the places you plan to visit, where you will stay, what kinds of activities you plan to do, and what you will eat.

IV. Class Activities

4-1. **Conversación en una agencia de viajes.** Imagine you are planning a vacation to a Spanish-speaking country and you visit a travel agency to find out where you might want to go. With a partner, prepare a dialogue between yourself and a travel agent in which he or she suggests Venezuela. You ask questions to find out about Venezuela since you are unfamiliar with this country. Ask about its weather and food, what to wear, activities, and currency. You end up convinced that Venezuela is the place to visit!